Between Tears
and Laughter

Lin Yutang

Must Have Books
503 Deerfield Place
Victoria, BC
V9B 6G5
Canada
trava2911@gmail.com

ISBN: 9781773236773

Copyright 2021 – Must Have Books

BETWEEN TEARS
AND LAUGHTER

"The Sage is one who has first discovered what is common in our hearts."

—MENCIUS

"O my friend, why do you, who are a citizen of the great and mighty and wise city of Athens, care so much about the laying up of the greatest amount of money and honor and reputation, and so little about wisdom and truth?"

—SOCRATES on trial

"The building of a peaceful world is not something to be accomplished by the writing of a treaty. It takes time to work out the relationships of men and women, but if we hope for peace, it must be done."

—ELEANOR ROOSEVELT

CONTENTS

PREFACE TO MYSELF

THE purpose of this book is to say something that must be said and say it with simplicity.

The age calls for simple statements and restatements of simple truths. The prophets of doom are involved, those who would bring light must be clear.

Our problem is the problem of moral decay and regeneration. From a handful of dust faith must come. There is more hope in a heather rose than in all the tons of Teutonic philosophy.

I do not know how to say these things, but God give me strength to say them.

The shadow of another war already looms before us. We have to think straight and think fast.

LIN YUTANG

I. THE SITUATION

1

A CONFESSION

AS I take up my pen to put down the thoughts bursting for expression in my head and my heart, I am troubled by the question of ruthless honesty and whether it is worth while. The question is not whether it is worth while to myself, but to the public. I have decided that it is worth while. For every good book is worth the reader's while when there is a real communion of the spirit, and this is possible only when he feels he is being taken into the author's confidence and the author is willing to reveal to him the innermost searchings of his heart and talk, as it were, in an unbuttoned mood, collar and tie loose, as by a friend's fireside. Nobody is ever misunderstood at a fireside; he may only be disagreed with. Agreement of opinion is the least important thing; disagreement is not only profitable, but necessary to thinking. At the fireside of a friend there is many a heated argument, after which both friends see many things not seen before. The writer who is willing to let go is sure of being understood, and only friendship which can stand occasional plain speaking is worth having.

I may as well make a confession here. For a month or so, I have been living in a daze. My mind, as I look back upon it now, has been a complete blank—I can only remember fuming and lying awake at night, thinking, thinking, thinking of how to break the solid wall of the Washington blockade of supplies for China. And thinking, lying awake at night, over the puzzle that President Roosevelt gave us. "Even now," said the President, "we are flying into China as much Lend-Lease material as ever traversed the Burma Road." That statement contained a joker, and I didn't like it—I didn't like joking and quibbling about vital supplies for my country at war. I knew the exact tonnage being flown in, which no official has dared to make public. It was the last straw, and broke the camel of easy-paced Chinese patience. It was a slap in the face, and stunned me into a half-daze.

Let me tell you how the Chinese camel broke. I had been slapped in the face before, or rather I felt China had been, successively. My country being pledged to a life-and-death struggle with Japan, these slaps were so personal that I felt as though someone had slapped me bodily. I have heard of prisoners being slapped by the Japanese, and have often wondered what Jesus would say about that. Jesus' injunctions ended with the second smiting on the left cheek; what one should do after turning the right cheek, if there was a third slap, followed by a fourth, the Bible did not tell us. Always it was not the injury, but the abuse, that hurt. What I could not stand was not selfishness—for that I could always understand; what I could not stand was bad manners. It was not so hard to be kicked unintentionally; it was harder to be told that being kicked didn't matter, or that the kicker had just never thought anything about it. I knew as well as any American that America was shipping oil and scrap iron to Tokyo to bomb Chinese women and children. Chinese patience is big enough for that. In a hypothetical case, if China should now declare herself a neutral and send scrap iron to Japan while the United States is fighting her, meanwhile maintaining a friendly relationship with the United States and praising her for her "heroic struggle," I doubt whether there would be as much equanimity in the American press or American diplomatic quarters as China showed before Pearl Harbor. But when President Roosevelt in the summer of 1941 called this policy of shipping iron and oil to Japan a "success," with evident satisfaction, that was the first big slap on my face. Of course all who hurt people with their words hurt through thoughtlessness. It obscured all the pin pricks before—the steady protests of the State Department to

Tokyo on the violation of U. S. property rights in China, on the damage to an American warehouse and three benches at Wuhu or a church building and four cats at Chinkiang, while ignoring the bombing of Chinese women.

The second slap came when the London Government ordered the Burma Road closed a second time. Since Britain, as events clearly demonstrated, neither meant for a moment to hold Burma with her own troops, nor would allow the entrance of Chinese troops, it was, in fact if not in name, an order to close the Burma Road. But then an English general gloated over the fall of Burma and expressed his "satisfaction" at the campaign which "gained three months for strengthening of India's defense."

The confiscation by General Wavell of China's Lend-Lease supplies arriving in India and Burma without previous notification of Chungking was a third slap.

The failure to make some slight effort to relieve the blockade of China by adequate air transport, and the obstructionist and dilly-dallying attitude of certain Washington bureaucrats in this matter, was a fourth big slap.

The shabby treatment accorded the Chinese Military Mission, sent to Washington to provide information and counsel in establishing a common war plan against Japan, was a fifth slap.

The smearing campaign about China's "fascism" and "imperialism" and "hoarding of supplies" as justification for not giving military aid to China—adding insult to injury—was a severe sixth slap.

Naturally, when, on top of all this, President Roosevelt put a joker in his statement about a perfect state of things regarding air transport to China, when it was actually scandalous and unprintable, the Chinese camel broke down. At least, as one Chinese, I did not think it was funny. . . . Further *double entendre* and lies about Stalin objecting to Chiang being invited to Casablanca kept me in that stunned condition for a month.

Then yesterday afternoon I took a walk in the uptown cross-streets, struggling with myself and striving for light to avoid a nervous collapse. I tried to see my own country as Americans would see her. Also I determined to view China's role across the decades. I arrived at two conclusions.

One of these conclusions, which had been slowly forming in my mind in the last month, was that China should travel the road with America and England in the next decades as a friendly nation, under two conditions. The first condition is that under whatever semblance or form of World Federation may be established, China will never, judging from her present experiences during the war, be accorded true equality, because she is Asiatic. She will be deprived of an air force of her own at the time the war stops, if her Allies can help it. She will not be accorded true equality until she is like Japan, twenty years from now, when she can build her own tanks and guns and battleships. When that time comes, there will be no need to argue about equality, such being the standards of the modern age. Meanwhile, acting with the traditional Chinese wisdom of "pretending to be a damn fool," China will be big enough for a few more insults and humiliations. Even Japan had to stand for the 5:5:3—for a time; the profound effect of this on Japanese psychology is deeper than westerners suspect, or can even understand. But there is the enormous patience, the bigness, the reasonableness of China. The second condition is that while acting as a friendly nation, China must learn the important lesson of acting for national self-interest as western nations have done and are doing. Such a friendly status should not prevent China from seeking her own profits and national strength as the only road to equality with the western powers, nor, if similar circumstances arose, should it prevent her from sending scrap iron and oil to the fighting enemies of her "friends," or closing her "friends'" strategic lines, in order to appease another powerful neutral.

I am convinced that this will be the shape of things, and will be the road China must travel before she will be treated as an equal, all talk of culture and friendship notwithstanding. For China, being newly initiated into the family of nations, is like a boy on his first day in school. His mother has told him to be polite and courteous to everybody so that his parents will not be ashamed of him. But I am the uncle who has been to such a school himself and who knows too well the ways and ethics of such schoolchildren. Seeing his nephew being beaten on his way home, the uncle takes off his coat and teaches the boy to hit back—as the only way to gain the respect of the fellow schoolboys. I would stop the boy from moping. . . . Who can tell me that the uncle's advice is wrong? From this conviction, I gained a certain strength, and I am not going to be upset by further slaps in the face before China reaches equality of arms, because I am expecting them as the natural law of modern world politics.

The second conclusion I arrived at was a mystic one. It was an intuition. I saw China growing strong, and Russia growing strong, and all Asia growing strong. I know that this nation of 450,000,000 people, united and awakened and purged by the war-fire, is coming up; the strength lies in her and nothing the western nations can do can stop her or keep her down.

From these reflections I regained my calm. Now I can be amused by these self-important nations who think they can dominate the world by sheer force, when Hitler has failed. I am no longer angry; only the stupidity of it all is a little boring. These thoughts blew like a whiff of clean air through the tortuous maze in which my will and my mind were imprisoned and paralyzed for a period. I came home, and ransacked the refrigerator, and laughed. My children said that a great change had come over me.

The human mind is a curious thing. It can take just so much and no more. In a recent discussion about bastards, my friends and I went over all the great talented bastards of history—not the "bastards" according to the New York taxi-drivers, which include all New York pedestrians. We discussed the social handicaps of illegitimate children, and how some succumbed and others by sheer force of character or intellect overcame them. Confucius was one; Ts'in Shih-huang, who built the Great Wall, was another. These became the tougher for what they had gone through. At a point, when the mind is strong enough, it always transcends the personal circumstances. Sometimes, provided the mind has sufficient moral and intellectual strength, it turns futile rage and scorn into a comedy of sparkling tears and laughter.

When such a mind comes into contact with the sordid realities of this world—its pomposities, hypocrisies, and stupidities —the sparks that are set forth produce a beautiful pattern. Now this I hold to be the function of the human mind—to set off sparks. When Dr. J. B. Watson and the host of scientific idiots picture the human mind as consisting merely of a set of reactions to dinner bells, instead of to ideas, idiosyncrasies, and vagaries of this blessed middle state, all you can do is to throw up your hands. . . .

So even in despair, man must laugh. The present world spectacle may be tragic. I share in all the depths of spiritual misery of this tragic decade. I do not believe in an automatic millennium that is going to blossom out of this spiritual desert. I smell too many corpses around. Human souls have smells as well as their bodies. Quite a few souls in a group identified by their love for Otto, Franco, and Hirohito have a smell that is distinctly stuffy. Others smell of the attic closet. This age is tragic, I admit. Is it not tragic, for example, that while in the last World War almost everyone believed it was the war to end all wars and wanted to make it so, now in this Second World War almost no writer that I have read dares even suggest that this is the war to end all wars, or act on that belief? We have lost the courage to hope.

The fonder you are of your ideals, the greater your heartbreaks. When you wish, for instance, that some slight but positive steps may be taken for the freedom of India, because India stands as the symbol of the issue of freedom for all nations, and that ideal is very dear and real to your heart, and somebody crushes that ideal like a flower, you feel a sort of pain.

But there is never a human tragedy but has its comic elements. There was probably never an age when the practical affairs of men did not look like a madhouse to some sane and perceptive minds, and there was never an age without its buffoons. In this connection I recall an excellent passage by Heinrich Heine in his *Reisebilder*:

> Yes, even in the highest pathos of the world tragedy, bits of fun slip in. . . . On this great stage of the world all passes exactly as on our beggarly boards. On it, too, there are tipsy heroes, kings who forget their parts, scenes which obstinately stay up in the air, prompters' voices sounding above everything, *danseuses* who create extraordinary effects with the poetry of their legs, and costumes, which are the main thing. And high in heaven, in the first row of the boxes, sit the dear little angels, and keep their lorgnettes on us comedians here down below, and the blessed Lord Himself sits seriously in His great box, and, perhaps, finds it dull, or calculates that this theater cannot be kept up much longer because this one gets too high a salary, and that one too little, and that they all play much too badly. . . .

Alas, our rulers are not gods, but puny, fallible men, like the kings who constantly forget their parts, and we common men should be their prompters. Sometimes, as on the American scene, while the pyrotechnics of Peyroutonism are going on, the American prompter's voice does seem to sound above everything. At heart, the prompters mean only well. And it is not in America alone that old actors tend to forget their lines; in the four corners of the earth, the play is not going too smoothly; and there seems to be a great deal of shouting and confusion over this scene in Spain, that scene in North Africa, and another scene in Austria in which the producer and the prompters cannot come to an agreement as to whether Otto of Hapsburg should step out on the boards or not, and still another scene of terrific confusion in India, where men fighting for freedom are fighting men fighting for their freedom.

And do not forget, prompters do help to save a performance. Old actors are forgetful creatures and a little prompting in time may yet help them to come off with a creditable performance. When the play is finished and the curtain rises again and again, the prompter is even willing to join in the applause and bring up the bouquets. But while the performance is going on, the prompter's heart is in his mouth when the actor goes on forgetting for a third and a fourth time, and does not even seem to understand the theme of the whole play. After the performance, the old actor will swear at the prompter in the wing, "You presumptuous, meddlesome fool! I knew perfectly well what I was doing." It is then up to the prompter to humor him by saying, "Of course you did. You were perfectly magnificent as ever, Horatio!"

So comedy is mixed with tragedy and the play goes on, and we see Eden and Hull rehearsing hurriedly, after the second act has opened, that scene about Russia which properly belonged to the prologue of the play. There are saints and sinners, and democrats and imperialists, and the imperialists are fighting for freedom and the democrats are fighting for empire, which means both are fighting to surrender their proper domains, or pretend to. Gandhi prays and fasts, which is such a curious act that no Christian can understand it, while Lord Halifax remarks that if he, as an Episcopalian, were to go up to the roof of the Viceroy's Palace to pray to God and fast, he would probably be sent to an insane asylum. There is Sir Norman Angell, hotly defending the right to freedom and the right of England in fighting the Indian right to freedom. I wonder what the dear little angels sitting in their front row boxes and looking down with their lorgnettes would do. I have a feeling that the year 1942 was the year in which the angels in heaven wept over their namesake on earth. If angels have tears. . . .

The time of world tragedy is hardly the time to laugh. But the prompter means well, even though if he shouts out too loud he contributes to the comedy, for there is something intrinsically funny about human mistakes. Every age has its buffoons and the buffoons make you laugh. Great men make great mistakes and small men make small mistakes. Then the great men love to point out the small mistakes of the small men, while they do not wish to have their great mistakes pointed out by the small men. A mistake is something which it is the privilege of the great men to commit and of the small men of this earth to point out after they are dead. Death comes and the buffoonery is over and we take the historical view. Dead men tell no tales and answer no arguments, and dead censors delete no passages from the books of posterity; so let them have the pleasure of deleting them now. We can already smile at the mistakes of Neville Chamberlain, the errors of the then popular national heroes of Versailles and of all the League of Nations officials in the last decade, because now the mistakes are irretrievable and pointing them out indicates a fine historical sense. On the assumption that all our dead ancestors and all the great statesmen of the earth are fools or buffoons except those still controlling our lives, we can go safely. The great thing about the teaching of history is that we must teach history but must not let history teach us.

Everything has its place and time. We men of the nineteen-forties can smile at the mistakes of the nineteen-thirties, and, in turn, the men of the nineteen-fifties will laugh at the mistakes of the nineteen-forties. It is this historical perspective that shall save us. When the war is over, the snails will be on the thorn, and the world will wag on, very much alive, as it always does, between tears and laughter. Sometimes there are more tears than laughter, and sometimes there is more laughter than tears, and sometimes you feel so choked you can neither weep nor laugh. For tears and laughter there will always be so long as there is human life. When our tear wells have run dry and the voice of laughter is silenced, the world will be truly dead.

2

KARMA

BUT if we take the historical perspective and view the development of human events, we are struck by a paradox which the science of human history so far has not been able to solve and the economic school of historians tend to ignore because they cannot make head or tail of it. That is the so-called "imponderables" of history. The word "ponder," I understand, comes from Latin *pondus* which means "weight," and "imponderable" means to me not so much something which we cannot ponder as something which we cannot measure or weigh. What a sad admission for the "scientists" of history! But there it is, a thing without weight or mass or shape or form.

Yet, while we may be perfectly contented with the facts and figures in contemporary events and policies, such as the number of dive bombers and tanks with which we know we are going to defeat Hitler, we get curiously spiritual when we view human events of the past across a stretch of decades. We run up constantly against these "imponderables," or "spiritual forces" or "psychological factors"—a kind of irreducible residuum which defies further scientific analysis. In other words, we are forced against our wish to accept a spiritual concept of history. But our temper of thinking is such that we hate anything which we cannot conveniently weigh or analyze or put in mathematical formulas. If we could have an electrometer to gauge the voltage of sentiments, we would immediately be able to understand them. As it is, with a sense of concession to an unconquerable enemy, we lay it in a corner of our laboratory, muttering something about not knowing what to do with "that puzzling substance."

So I must speak of "Karma." The Hindus have evolved a perfect theory of the law of moral action, and you can understand this law of moral action only when you take the historical perspective. Briefly, it is the theory that we are responsible for our moral thoughts and actions, that these thoughts and actions have a causal relationship with the past and the future, and that we cannot escape from the chain of causation. It is almost like the law of cause and effect in physical motion, and the law of the indestructibility of matter and energy in the physical universe. We have nothing remotely comparable with it. The very fact that popular Christianity, as well as popular Buddhism, seeks this balance of rewards and punishments in the future life shows that they do not recognize, and are not aware of, the adequate principle of moral causation in this present life.

Reading President Roosevelt's speech on Lincoln's Birthday I found that Lincoln was a Brahmin; in fact anyone who believes in the persistence of the effects of our thoughts and actions is a Brahmin. There was a quotation from Lincoln given at the end of Roosevelt's radio broadcast:

Fellow citizens, we cannot escape history. We of this Congress and of this administration will be remembered in spite of ourselves. No personal significance or insignificance can spare one or another of us. The fiery trial through which we pass will light us, in honor or dishonor, to the latest generation.

Abraham Lincoln happened to state the principles of Karma accurately and adequately in this single passage. *"We cannot escape history"*: that is Karma. Lincoln might have said in 1862, "The sounds which I am uttering now vanish apparently into thin air, yet they persist into eternity. If we had a scientific apparatus delicate and sensitive enough to catch and record these sound waves, which we don't, we might find that these sounds stretch into the eternity of space. Similarly, with our moral actions." *"We will be remembered in spite of ourselves"*: that is inescapability. *"No personal significance or insignificance will spare one or another of us"*: even the smallest act has its consequences. *"Light us to the latest generation"*: the effect is practically eternal, through effects producing further effects. *"In honor and dishonor"*: we bear the dead weight of the past and carry in ourselves its shames and its glories. In other words, the moment we live in is a causal and indissoluble link between yesterday and tomorrow. The word "now" has mathematically no meaning and no boundary: some time elapses between my writing the first letter "n" and the last letter "w." The stream of time is carrying us forward; we live between yesterday and tomorrow.

In the light of this Brahmin theory, the thesis "Let's win the war first and talk of what we are fighting for afterwards" simply does not make sense. Time refuses to be cut up like this. "Win-the-War-First" Churchill's dictum is philosophic nonsense, based on the grip of inertia of the past and fear of the future. It is based on his complete unwillingness to escape from the past and his great desire to escape from the future. One must live in mortal terror of the peace to refuse to think about or discuss the postwar problems. I know and I notice that even W-t-W-F Churchill is forced, as time goes on, to discuss the status of the British colonies and of Polish frontiers before he can see his way to win the war. Meanwhile the time machine, the wheel of Karma, is carrying Churchill forward, as a spring torrent carries a leaf swiftly and surely toward an overflooded dam. Sooner or later, it will reach that much feared overflooded dam of peace—unless it is left behind by time.

There is a law in physics that "action and reaction are equal." It has a certain awe-inspiring simplicity, like the law of universal gravitation. It takes some courage to state simple things like that, but back of it are some complicated mathematical equations, probably twenty-seven letters long, that the layman cannot handle and does not even suspect. The similar law that action and reaction are equal in the realm of moral action is equally subtle, but less capable of mathematical proof. The Buddhist doctrine is that Karma is "cumulative," that it is something that is accumulated day by day and year by year by our little acts and our secret thoughts, almost like physical momentum that one gains or loses by little acts, hesitations, and delays. This Karma carries one along toward a future situation—eventually salvation or death. Buddha himself states it in plain psychological terms when he says in the opening sentences of the Dhammapada:

All that we are is the result of what we have thought: it is founded on our thoughts, it is made up of our thoughts. If a man speaks or acts with an evil thought, pain follows him, as the wheel follows the foot of the ox that draws the carriage.

All that we are is the result of what we have thought: it is founded on our thoughts, it is made up of our thoughts. If a man speaks or acts with a pure thought, happiness follows him, like a shadow that never leaves him.

This sort of teaching requires a little Hindu imagination which conceives of moral things almost as real as physical things. If we could give our moral self a body, we would find that body consists of ganglions of our thoughts, acting like vaso-motor nerves producing muscular actions. The sum of such actions acting on the persons themselves and on fellow human beings would produce the momentum of human events and determine the future situation of the human world and of the individual selves. Evil breeds sorrow and good breeds happiness, as inevitably and as accurately as one billiard ball sets another rolling at a particular angle and with a particular force. That is the theory of moral responsibility of all human acts and thoughts, and that is what the Buddhists mean by the Wheel of the Law ("Dharma"), and again, in a more pathetic sense, by the Wheel of Karma.

We have to be satisfied with some such statement of the moral laws of the universe. It has sufficient austerity and rigor about it, which is what we want. We are used to economic thinking. Bales of cotton and marginal excess of exports over imports and lowering and raising of tariffs are easy and clear to handle mentally; there is something neat and tidy about them. "Bales of cotton" makes sense, but "bales of good will and co-operation" rarely does, and we dislike hazy, unclear thinking. Once in a while, however, our politicians leave this comfortable realm and, by lapses of thinking, launch forth into abstract phrases like "the unconquerable spirit of man against oppression" and the "force of the human love for freedom," and the public grows a little restive with the lushness and emotion. Then, by further lapses of memory, our columnists and publicists once in a while further indulge in terms like "the invisible forces of history" and the "psychological factors" and the "imponderables" as if they were real things.

The fact is, we hate to ponder over the imponderables. The more we ponder over them, the more cloudy or confused our thoughts become, and the very realistic and straight-thinking lobbyists and Senators soon call us down for handing out sentimental stuff and rubbish. Secretly, we feel a little ashamed of ourselves and a little sheepish for committing such sins of the spirit, and we make a resolution to talk of tariff quotas and stick to brass tacks next time, and, God willing, we shall succeed. Wrecked reputations can still be salvaged if we talk next time in hard-hitting terms that this age can understand. Raise the standard of living, for instance—sheer physical, animal living—or minimum wage standards and guaranteed income. Nobody will misunderstand that. Eventually everything comes back in terms of gold, unless it is silver, for we are living in the Golden Age. All that glitters is not gold: there is antimony and tungsten, but at least there is a price for it.

That explains our impatience with lush sentimentality. But there are many things we have to do with that we can neither weigh nor measure nor even prove. The dignity of the individual, for instance, and the idea of equality and freedom, can never be proved, for science can never prove that the individual is dignified or even free. On the contrary, if science is science, it can only prove there is no such thing as freedom, or where would be the prestige of the mechanical laws? These things forever elude us, but held at a respectable distance and clothed in eerie shapes, their presence nevertheless seems real. In our forgetful and less scientific and mathematical moments, we know they have a meaning, an existence behind a veil, a shape that comes up behind us on a silent night as we are sitting by the fireside and suddenly puts its hands across our eyes and whispers, "Guess who?" Persistently these shapes come to haunt us. Only to the spiritual thinkers do they become real, almost with a weight and mass and form.

The Indian conception of Karma somewhat scares us with its exactitude. Truth pays (it makes us happy) and justice pays, and, if Indian metaphysics is right, freedom of the soul pays enormous dividends. Actually Buddha and the Brahmins never talked so vulgarly, but they meant substantially the same thing. We are willing to consider the imponderables if we can be made to see that they produce results, sometimes very important results, and if we can prove that action and reaction are equal in the moral as well as the physical realm. And so the word "Karma" has come to mean for me a means of restating a spiritual concept of history, of asserting the reality of moral causes and effects over against economic causes and remedies. Unless this is understood, our discussion of peace and war can never rise above the level of swine-and-slop economics.

The China war is a fairly good illustration of the law of Karma—for the present called "imponderables." The strength of Chinese resistance can be proved to be equal to the measure of the enormities of Japan's previous acts. It is of the very essence of Karma that we must speak of its "cumulative" effect over a period of years or decades, until it is finally shown in visible events. Whence arose that great moral force which united the common people of China against the Japanese and precluded the desertion of local generals to the invader's side, which was commonly believed possible?

This force can be understood only as reaction to the sum total of Japan's previous acts. To mention only a few in this series: the Twenty-One Demands of 1915; the overt intention to rape Shantung at the Versailles Conference; the rape of Manchuria in 1931; the Shanghai War of 1932; the brazen and shameless wholesale smuggling of Japanese goods under Japanese army and consular protection in North China in the years 1932-1936; the encroachment on Chahar in 1933-1934; the sneak attempt to penetrate Inner Mongolia in 1936. All through the years 1931-1937, anti-Japanese demonstrations were suppressed in China. But the emotional reaction, though invisible, steadily accumulated and accounts today for the inner strength and stubbornness and unity of Chinese resistance. Furthermore, according to the law of Karma, no small act, however insignificant, happened without sending a ripple through the following decades. Such a local happening as cutting off the nose and ears and gouging out the eyes of a Chinese diplomatic official, Tsai Kung-shih, Chinese Foreign Commissioner at Tsinan in 1928, left its imprint on the Chinese mind and spirit as much as the wholesale rape and slaughter at Nanking in 1937. The Japanese thought that the "episode" ended with the official "closing of the incident"; the Karma theory says it did not. The Japanese could not escape history, nor could the Chinese. Briefly, that was why the Chinese and the Japanese had to fight. "A small injustice can be drowned in wine," says a Chinese writer, "but a great wrong can be restituted only by the sword." Here moral causes and effects are immensely real.

The same is true of the war in the West. If someone could gauge the voltage generated in 130,000,000 American breasts by the Pearl Harbor attack, he could be almost certain that the moral effect was as disastrous for Japan as the physical effect was militarily advantageous for her at the initial stage of the war. But it is exactly such generated voltage that our diplomats and army men despise and ignore when they start out like small men to direct the greatest campaign of world history.

There are a rhythm and a pattern of things in human history if only we could detect them. I understand that X-ray pictures showing strains caused by impact on metal and lucite reveal highly interesting patterns which the naked human eye cannot see. And I am told by anti-vegetarians that when we cut up a radish, the agony of its spirit is shown in an outrageous emitting of electric currents that must be a scream. We cannot hear the scream of the radish, nor could Hitler reckon the "karmatic" currents set up by outraged and cut-up Europe. But history will make these plain enough in time when their effects become evident. And Hitler is not going to escape history. In other words, he is not going to escape the Wheel of Karma. I really wish Hitler were a Buddhist. He would have been a little more subtle. What the Germans never really understand is metaphysics, all Teutonic tomes to the contrary.

It is, however, not Hitler alone who ignores the karmatic currents of history. We of the Allied nations do not admit that such karmatic currents of "imponderables" exist, and we are not providing for them, being contented on the strictly swine-and-slop level of war and peace planning. We simply have no conception of Karma. Economics makes no distinction between human mouths and pigs' snouts, and all the charts and dissertations on food and populations and tariffs are no more than the counting of snouts. The idea is that if you segregate the hogs in different sties and throw in enough hog fodder, with the fences neither too high nor too low between them, the hogs are going to live in peace, and then a millennium will descend upon the earth.

3

THE EMERGENCE OF ASIA

MEANWHILE the Wheel of Karma grinds on, which is my way of saying that invisible forces of history are breaking up the international structure of this world. Politically, we ignore them. We are acting in this war as if these forces did not exist. The laws of Karma can never be defied or nullified. We are sowing what we do not mean to reap.

The one great fact in this world war is the emergence of Russia and of Asia, but we prefer to ignore it. I have made a passing discourteous reference to Sir Norman Angell. As a European liberal, he is probably as good as any. But as a European liberal, his liberal concepts of the necessity of world co-operation and standing and falling together are strictly "white" and limited to west of the Suez Canal, and specifically to a refurbished form of "Union Now" with England. His notion of Russia and of Asia stands intellectually on a par with the Tory Lady Astor, who says, "I would like China and Russia to be in the framework of a new society formed by America and the British Commonwealth, but they would have to get into the 'British way of thinking.'" Such superb gems can only be cut in London. The following mathematical riddle has always puzzled me: if the diameter of the human skull is five inches five, but the thickness of its sides is also five inches five, what is the empty space in between?

The nineteenth-century world structure is crumbling, and an Empire breaks—unwillingly. If one could see the invisible forces rising and risen in Asia, one would be forced to look upon this Second World War as a revolution in the world structure. *This revolution is being forced by Asia upon Europe, and not by Europe upon Asia.* For verily, we are witnessing the birth pangs of a new earth, without being sure of the "birth of a new freedom." The forces of a rising Asia are steadily moving on.

Japan is trying to force a revision of the world map by battle. China is forcing a revision of Asiatic roles in world politics by enormous hope and self-reliance. India is trying, futilely, to force a revision by addressing prayers to air patrols and riot squads and the flogging whip. The lack of vision on the part of the Allied leaders, however, has compelled them to fly in the teeth of this Wheel of Karma. And not in Asia alone, but throughout the earth, forces are rising, growing, to demand that birth of a new freedom of which Abraham Lincoln prophetically spoke, so that the world shall not be "half-free and half-slave." These forces are causing a dislocation of our general ideas and traditions. But being unprepared and caught unready, we are meeting them, not with clarity and simplicity and strength, but in utter confusion. The first principles being not yet established, we are lost in a desert of temporizing ingenuities.

I do not often quote Jesus, but I must quote him this time.

When ye see a cloud rise out of the west, straightway ye say, There cometh a shower; and so it is, And when ye see the south wind blow, ye say, There will be heat; and it cometh to pass. Ye hypocrites, ye can discern the face of the sky and of the earth; but how is it that ye do not discern this time?

The emergence of Asia—and I think of Russia as half-Asiatic —is the one greatest single fact of this war. It has upset the war schedule and is going to upset the peace schedule. It will upset everything in fact except Lady Astor's imperturbable "British way of thinking." If we don't look out, the mesmeric powers of Lady Astor's "way of thinking" can think the world revolution to a stop. But it is my belief that even if we wanted a modified survival of the nineteenth-century fabric in the form of a fairly white domination of the world, it is now a little too late. Asia is too aroused to submit and too big to spank. The West must either plan for co-operation with Asia or plan without it and make ready for a bigger and better war.

Ernest Hemingway, on his return from China, quoted a Chinese officer as saying, "You know why the Englishman wears a monocle? With one eye, he sees what he wants to see and with the other eye he does not see what he does not want to see." German officers wear monocles, also. But that is also why monocles can never be popular in the United States or in China. Lady Astor really means that the Russians and Chinese should wear British monocles, but we happen to dislike them, and so do the Russians. So it seems there is little chance of seeing "Russia and China in the framework of a new society formed by America and the British Commonwealth." As a Chinese, I would rather hang the new society and keep my binocular vision.

The emergence of Asia simply means this: *the end of the era of imperialism.* Nothing is going to stop it. To keep up the nineteenth-century system, the white man would have to strangle Russia and China. Now it is a little too late. The West may still try, as Professor Nicholas John Spykman bravely advises: "It is well to remember that, whatever may ultimately be achieved in the form of integration and federation, we will start more or less where we left off. Unless the United States continues to struggle until she has defeated not only her enemies [Germany and Japan] but also her former allies [Russia and China], the postwar period will begin with an international society composed of numerous independent states"—which is what Professor Nicholas John Spykman dares not contemplate. Am I to suppose that this is the type of political doctrine being taught in American college classrooms? I remember, during World War I, the term "power politics" used to be written as *Machtpolitik* and had a German flavor; now it is not necessary—Germany has conquered us from within.

The fact is, that, granted a little common intelligence in the racial make-up, any nation will come up in time. How did nineteenth-century imperialism begin, and how did the white man go about conquering the world, and what made him think he was superior to the other peoples? Because the white man had guns, and the Asiatics had none. The matter was as simple as that. Study the Boxer War and the Sino-French war of the nineteenth century. Chinese soldiers in those days carried umbrellas and brandished knives; many others were archers. Only in the first decade of the twentieth century did we hear of Yüan Shih-kai's "New Army," and by the "New Army" we simply meant that his soldiers were the only ones who had rifles. If the comparison is disillusioning, let us even assume that one army had fowling pieces and the other had Krupp rifles.

If my reader is still following me, he can at once see that the only logical way to keep Asia down permanently would be to keep the knowledge of the use of rifles and guns from the Asiatics as we are trying to keep the American bomb sight from the enemy. Stretch it across the decades, and you know it cannot be done. For a century that discrepancy in arms alone maintained the white empires in Asia. What the great Second World War suddenly revealed is that now the Japanese, the Chinese, and the Russians all have guns. This fact is going to change world history; the discrepancy no longer exists. What is more, the Japanese can fight as well as the white men; so can the Russians; so can the Chinese. They are all fighting. Now what? Disarm them? Police them? Keep them down by Culbertson's "quota principle" like the quota principle of 5:5:3 for British, U. S., and Japanese navies at the Washington Conference?

The white man's mission has become a paradox and a boomerang. The white man gave the yellow man the Bible and guns. He should have given him the Bible, which he himself had no use for, and kept from him the guns that he himself used most expertly. He thought that if he shot a few yellow men on earth after his missionaries had saved their souls for heaven, that ought to make it even. But he was mistaken. Now the yellow man has learned to take the Bible as seriously as his white brother, and I am sure the sons of Satan, yellow and white, well equipped with tommy guns, will plunge this world into another orgy of blood. That is to say, if we are naïve enough to think that all we need to do is to transfer the standards of Europe to Asia and impose the white man's power politics on a world scale, we shall have the whole world, instead of Europe, as an arena of periodic bloodshed and slaughter.

I am sure that all "progressive-thinking" people, including some professors, are thinking in this direction. The beautiful pattern of European chaos, its standards and its ethics, will become the pattern for the future world: all Hottentots will have a quart of milk a day; the Hindus are to put on collar and tie; Madagascans are to go to church; and the world is to be thankful for it. That is the white man's mission and the boon European civilization will confer upon the world, only with a few periodic volcanic eruptions, it is admitted, whose hot lava of destruction will run over some village in Guadalcanal or Burma. On the other hand, he is going to have a quart of milk a day. Is that not a bargain?

Our present solution for the changed world picture is in fact quite simple. The white man is saying to all the other races of the world: "I am trying to be perfect even as our Father in Heaven is perfect, but all you natives need to do is to be perfect like me and get into my way of thinking, and I am sure our Father in Heaven will be quite pleased with you. He wouldn't mind if you had a little heavier pigment. Now toddle along." That is the New Jerusalem according to Lady Astor, Clarence Streit, and Sir Norman Angell.

4

THE SUICIDE OF GREECE

THE solution for the international problems arising out of the emergence of Asia suggested in the previous chapter does not seem satisfactory or attractive to me. International suicide is never attractive.

Herr Professor Nicholas John Spykman prefers a heroic, uninterrupted march of the United States of America to world supremacy by just a couple of more wars in which she shall continue to struggle until she crushes only a couple of hundred million Russians and only four or five hundred million Chinese. . . . He prefers this to the unthinkable alternative of "an international society composed of numerous independent states." I prefer the latter. The Spenglerian gloom of Spykman's prophetic and professorial voice is after all depressing; we common men should be a little more cheerful. What Spykman means is simply that western civilization had better commit suicide as Pericles' Athenian Empire did. Let's be a little learned and professorial and tiresome and go back to Thucydides.

Greece perished because she failed to solve the problem of empire versus freedom. European civilization must also perish if it fails to solve the problem of empire versus freedom. How perdition will come about we cannot foretell like Nostradamus. But the by-plays of the conflict of forces and the episodes and the different phases of development, which may take generations for us but are only moments in the eyes of God or of mankind's history, will be essentially the same as those that brought about the suicide of the Greek world.

There are too many similarities. The advantage of delving into Thucydides is that there the picture is focused into a smaller and simpler scale, its geography is foreshortened in space, and its half-century of conflict and decay is now conveniently foreshortened in time. Briefly, it was the conflict of Athenian sea power and Spartan land power, and the sad story of the failure of moral leadership. The dream of an All-Greek Federation petered out, owing to that moral failure and to the unwillingness or incapacity of Athens to solve the problem of empire versus freedom. We are wise after the fact and can put our finger on the arrogance and stupidity of the Athenians as the psychological cause of that failure. Let us only hope that the dream of world federation may have less the character of the Delian Confederacy, and that there be no Alexander from across the mountains to descend upon and desolate the Ionian plains and wipe out what was a world of glorious human achievements. The tragic motivation of that historical drama was that the heroine, Athens, democratic and brilliant and arrogant, loved freedom for herself, but could not understand the equally passionate love of freedom of the other Greek cities.

Reading history sometimes gives one a curious feeling in the pit of the stomach. For the similarities to the modern world are rather alarming. Unquestionably the Athenians were democrats; but unfortunately, democracies could also commit suicide. Human art had never soared higher than in Athens; the

light of sweet reason and a wide-awake curiosity had illumi-
nated her mind, and simplicity and harmony had beautified
her spirit. Athenian pride was justifiable. Modern presidents
can boast of no greater achievements in their democracies,
or in modern civilization in general, than Pericles did of the
achievements of the Athenian way of life in his Funeral Speech
in honor of the fallen heroes at the end of the first year of the
Peloponnesian War. The tone is strikingly like an American
Presidential Address.

Before I praise the dead, I should like to point out by
what principles of action we rose to power, and under
what institutions and through what manner of life our
empire became great. . . . Our form of government does
not enter into rivalry with the institutions of others. We
do not copy our neighbors, but we are an example to them.
It is true that we are called a democracy, for the administration is in the hands of the many and not of the few.
But while the law secures justice for all alike in private
disputes, the claim of excellence is also recognized; and
when a citizen is distinguished, he is preferred to the
public service, not as a matter of privilege, but as a reward
of merit. Neither is poverty a bar, but a man may benefit
his country whatever be the obscurity of his condition.
. . . While we are thus unconstrained in our private
intercourse, a spirit of reverence pervades our public acts;
we are prevented from doing wrong by respect for author-
ity and for the laws, having especial regard to those un-
written laws which bring upon the transgressor of them
the reprobation of the general sentiment.
And we have not forgotten to provide for our weary
spirits many relaxations from toil; we have regular games
and sacrifices throughout the year; at home the style of
life is refined; and the delight which we daily feel in all
these things helps to banish melancholy. Because of the

greatness of our city, the fruits of the whole earth flow
in upon us; so that we enjoy the goods of other countries
as freely as of our own. . . . And in the matter of education, whereas they [the "Nazi" Spartans] from early
youth are always undergoing laborious exercises which are
to make youth brave, we live at ease, and yet are equally
ready to face the perils which they face. . . .[1]

Pericles could not have spoken better if he were giving a
speech in honor of the heroes fallen at Guadalcanal. He could
write the Thanksgiving Proclamation for 1943 in exactly the
same words. For here is the essence of democracy as Pericles
perceived it and as Thucydides reported it from memory (and
his own imagination), and in the exact terms in which a *New
York Times* editorial might have put it:

For we are lovers of the beautiful, yet with economy, and
we cultivate the mind without loss of manliness. . . . An
Athenian citizen does not neglect the state because he takes
care of his own household; and even those of us who are
engaged in business have a very fair idea of politics. We
alone regard a man who takes no interest in public affairs,
not as a harmless, but as a useless character; and if few of
us are originators, we are all sound judges of a policy.
The great impediment to action is, in our opinion, not
discussion, but want of that knowledge which is gained by
discussion preparatory to action. For we have a peculiar
power of thinking before we act and of acting too, whereas
other men are courageous from ignorance. . . . To sum
up: I say that Athens is the school of Hellas, and that the
individual Athenian in his own person seems to have the
power of adapting himself to the most varied forms of
action with the utmost versatility and grace. . . . I have

---

[1] Thucydides, *Peloponnesian War*, Bk. II, Ch. 36-39.

dwelt upon the greatness of Athens because I want to show you that we are contending for a higher prize than those who enjoy none of these privileges. . . .[2]

There was never a clearer defense of the strength of Athenian democracy and of the Athenian way of life. Unfortunately, it was an imperialist democracy, and the Greek world remained half-slave and half-free. Athens had survived her "Great War I"—the Persian Wars and the defeat at Salamis; it was rather the failure of moral leadership, the arrogance and stupidity of the Athenians in failing to recognize the principle of freedom and equality for all Greek cities, that led to incessant wars and the final catastrophe. In the words of Professor Godolphin:

> Athenian control of the Delian Confederacy after the Persian Wars brought Greece face to face with another great problem of the fifth century, the conflict between an imperialist democracy based on maritime power and a conservative aristocracy based on military superiority. The exhaustion produced by the Peloponnesian War, the inadequacy of any Greek State as leader, combined with the failure of Pan-Hellenism and the chronic inability of the Greeks to create a genuine federation, leads to the political solution of the fourth century.[3]

—Which was suicide.

One could wish that Athenian and modern parallels were less exact. On the basis that human chicanery, the play of power politics, and the emotions of jealousy and fear are the same in all ages, Thucydides was quite right in his predictions. "But if he who desires a true picture of the events which have happened, and *of the like events which may be expected to happen hereafter in the course of human things,* shall pro-

---

[2] *Ibid.,* Bk. II, Ch. 40-42.
[3] Francis R. B. Godolphin, Introduction to *The Greek Historians,* pp. XIX-XX.

nounce what I have written to be useful, then I shall be satisfied."

The parallels are in fact uncomfortably and alarmingly exact. Athens was a democracy. It was a sea power, fighting the land power of Sparta. Will Durant expresses the situation well:

> But the basic cause of the war was the growth of the Athenian Empire, and the development of Athenian control over the commercial and political life of the Aegean. Athens allowed free trade there in time of peace, but only by Imperial sufferance; no vessel might sail that sea without her consent. . . . Athens defended this domination as a vital necessity; she was dependent upon imported food, and was determined to guard the routes by which that food came. In policing the avenues of international trade Athens performed a real service to peace and prosperity in the Aegean, but the process became more and more irksome as the pride and wealth of the subject cities grew.[4]

She enforced extraterritoriality upon the other Greek cities; any case involving Athenians arising within the Confederacy had to be tried at Athenian courts; only Athenian justice was good enough, although no one need imagine that the Athenian jurors were internationally minded liberals devoid of a hidden warmth for their fellow citizens and of contempt for the aliens.

The federation on a basis of freedom and equality which was the only hope for survival of the Greek world had degenerated into a farce. For under whatever form and whatever name, Athens had to dominate the Greek world. She had to control the fleet created in the name of the Confederacy for the common defense of the Greek states against aggressors and international brigands. Only such an international police could enforce international peace in the Aegean Sea. It became such a farce that Athens *coerced* others to join the League and

---

[4] Will Durant, *Life of Greece*, p. 439.

demolished the other cities that refused to join, for common protection, what was now frankly and unashamedly called her "empire."

> If we may believe Thucydides [says Will Durant], the democratic leaders of Athens, while making liberty the idol of their policy among Athenians, frankly recognized that the Confederacy of free cities had become an empire of force . . . *the inherent contradiction between the worship of liberty and the despotism of empire co-operated with the individualism of the Greek states to end the Golden Age.*[5]

Thucydides, an Athenian, was ingenuous and impartial enough to tell us that the real cause of the Peloponnesian War was the domination of Athenian power. The Athenians were determined to enforce a *Pax Athenica*. They were for free trade, being themselves dependent upon imported grains from Egypt and Thrace, and were modern enough to enforce economic sanctions. Megara rebelled and helped Athen's enemy, Corinth. Pericles ordered all Megarian products excluded from Attica and the Empire. Megara and Corinth appealed to Sparta. Sparta intervened, and demanded the repeal of the embargo. Pericles agreed, but demanded in return the throwing open of Spartan cities to foreign trade. Sparta agreed, but countered with the demand that Athens acknowledge the full independence of all Greek cities. Pericles, however, refused to preside over the liquidation of the Athenian Empire. Thereupon Sparta declared war. Writes Thucydides, "The real though unavowed cause I believe to have been the growth of the Athenian power, which terrified the Lacedaemonians and forced them into war: but the reasons publicly alleged on either side were as follows . . ."[6] i.e., quite different.

---

[5] *Ibid.*, p. 440.
[6] *Peloponnesian War*, Bk. I, Ch. 23.

It is therefore correct to say that it was Pericles' Athens that ruined the Grecian world, and that the love of power and commercial imperialism were the causes of war—in ancient as in modern times. Athenian arrogance and love of power resulted in a pattern of power politics very similar to that of the present day—disaffection of allies, coercion in times of strength and cajolery in moments of weakness, shifting alliances and counteralliances, internecine wars, and final exhaustion and ruin. Will Durant's judgment was as follows:

> Under him [Pericles] Athens had reached her zenith; but because her height had been attained in part through the wealth of an unwilling confederacy, and through power that invited almost universal hostility, the Golden Age was unsound in its foundations, and was doomed to disaster when Athenian statesmanship failed in the strategy of peace.[7]

We would be naïve if we believed that the problem of an imperialist democracy was new and peculiar to the modern world. The Athenians were thoroughly familiar with the principles of power politics and the doctrine of force. They knew imperialist prestige hinged upon "firmness" in dealing with subject cities. That "firmness," no less than that of the Viceroy of India, was shown in her dealings with cities that demanded freedom, and the firmness demanded the massacre of all male adults of a rebellious Melos and selling their women and children as slaves, much as they prized "freedom" and "democracy" for themselves. It demanded the slaughter of 1,000 ringleaders of the Mytilene rebellion; the logic of imperialism demanded it. Said Cleon to the Athenian Assembly, "You should remember that your empire is a despotism exercised over unwilling subjects who are always conspiring against you; they do not obey in return for any kindness which you do them

---

[7] *Life of Greece*, p. 442.

to your own injury, but only in so far as you are their master; they have no love for you, but they are held down by force." [8]

Gifted with lucid reasoning, the Athenians could make a no less eloquent defense of power politics and "expediency" against "honor" than ourselves. In the famous debate between the Athenians and the Melians, the former said:

> But you and we should say what we really think, and aim only at what is possible, for we both alike know that into the discussion of human affairs the question of justice only enters where the pressure of necessity is equal, and that *the powerful exact what they can, and the weak grant what they must.* . . . Of the gods we believe, and of man we know, that by a law of their nature wherever they can rule they will. This law was not made by us, and we are not the first who have acted on it; we did but inherit it, and shall bequeath it to all time, and we know that you and all mankind, if you were as strong as we are, would do as we do. [9]

Ribbentrop or Lord Linlithgow could not have improved upon this.

The innate belief in force was the reason why Athenian statesmanship failed in its strategy for peace. The Greeks did believe in a sort of Karma in the form of "Nemesis"; retribution followed *hybris,* "insolent violence." The Greek dramatists played upon the theme of the vengeful Nemesis of insolent success, but in international politics they were as good as blind, though no blinder than we are today.

There is something comically Aesopian in that debate between the Athenians and the Melians, the former trying by threat and cajolery to induce the latter to join their "World Union," and the latter praying to the former like mice praying

---

[8] *Peloponnesian War,* Bk. III, Ch. 37.
[9] *Ibid.,* Bk. V. Ch. 89 and 105.

to a cat to be denied the pleasure of physical absorption into
the belly of the Athenian she-cat. Substitute the Hindus today
for the Melians and we have a Thucydidean picture of modern
politics:

> *Melians:* It may be to your interest to be our masters,
> but how can it be ours to be your slaves?
> *Athenians:* To you the gain will be that by submission
> you will avert the worst; and we shall be the richer for
> your preservation.
> *Melians:* But must we be your enemies? Will you not
> receive us as friends if we are neutral and remain at peace
> with you?
> *Athenians:* No, your enmity is not half as mischievous
> to us as your friendship; for the one is in the eyes of our
> subjects an argument of our power, the other of our weak-
> ness.[10]

After Winston Churchill had made a speech in the House
of Commons on March 17, 1943 supporting Mr. Stanley, Secretary of State for Colonies, John Dugdale, Laborite, asked
whether he was aware that Mr. Stanley's "somewhat truculent
speech created misgivings both in the United States and the
Dominions." The Prime Minister responded, "We must equally
beware of truculence and of grovelling."

That Thucydides could analyze the psychological motives
of our modern statesmen so skillfully is merely evidence that
ancient and modern men are essentially alike. Yielding and
compromise would be construed as a sign of "weakness," even
when Socrates chose to give himself thirty days to die. The
seventy-year-old Socrates happened to believe in *satyagraha,* and
in the integrity of spiritual principles. His accuser, Anytus,
stood for law and order and even for public morality. Anytus
went to the temple to worship. Anytus, too, was a good man,

[10] *Ibid.,* Bk. V. Ch. 92-95.

and a God-fearing man, by all public records. There was another good man, Pontius Pilate, who once washed his hands of an important matter. Who ever said that Pontius Pilate was a bad man? He merely declined diplomatically to interfere in the private affairs of another nation, even though it involved the murder of an innocent man. There are in fact more historic analogies than we can stomach.

5

CHURCHILL AND PERICLES

READING history may be a costly effort. *Thucydides* in the Modern Library costs 95 cents, but the failure to read it properly máy be much more costly to the modern world. For today the issue of empire versus freedom is unsolved and ignored. Therefore the issue of India as a test case must be studied.

The issue of India is more than the issue of India; it is the issue of freedom and what we intend to do with it. Because we will not even face the issue of empire versus freedom, we have come to the perfectly anomalous position which bothers anybody but an Englishman, that in this war of freedom the Indian fighters for freedom are in jail for committing the crime of fighting for freedom.

Freedom—what magic in that word! Let Freedom ring! But Freedom must doff the *sari* and wear a European gown before we can love her. There is the English freedom which we associate with cozy English cottages and beautiful lawns and the Lake District, and there is the Indian freedom riding on an elephant in the Indian jungle. Men's minds are limited and cannot see that she whom we love wears but a thin white muslin veil around her body, and wraps herself neither in a Union

Jack nor in a loincloth. She dwells in the hearts of man and can be seen only with the eye of the mind.

So the English are fighting to be free and at the same time fighting the Indians who are fighting to be free, and the Indians are fighting to be free in order to help the English fighting to be free in this war for freedom. This has become such a confounded mess that if the Englishman in India ever thinks, he ought to die of apoplexy. I have no fear that he will. One just does not discuss the Four Freedoms in India, nor hear them mentioned. It is a little awkward, isn't it? Win the war first and use your brains afterward. Only a robust English mind can survive these logical inconsistencies, and I have no doubt it will. You are sure of it when you hear the tone of satisfaction in the Viceroy of India's report on killings in India: 940 killed, 1,630 injured, 60,229 arrested, 26,000 convicted, 18,000 detained without trial—since August, 1942. As a correspondent in the *New Republic* puts it, "the Viceroy reports it like so many stuck hogs on line in a Chicago packinghouse." Every one of those hogs is a fighter for freedom, and not afraid to be beaten, flogged, or sent to jail for it. A hog is a hog, or ain't it?

I have recently acquired, undeservedly, a reputation for being "anti-English," at least among a few ladies in New York, because I spoke for the freedom of India as if I meant it. What the connection between the two is, I have utterly failed to see, and my lady friends are not able to enlighten me. My position is quite clear: I am not anti-English; I am anti-idiots of any nationality, including my own. I am not just against Churchill's Tory policy toward India—I detest it. That Churchill is English I know, but to me that is entirely incidental; I should detest that India policy whether its author were an Englishman, a Frenchman, a Jap, or a Chinese. I happen to be able to distinguish English Tories and liberals, and I happen to like the Archbishop of Canterbury better than Winston Churchill.

When two Englishmen hold opposite views, like the British

Prime Minister and the Archbishop of Canterbury, American editors think it is their duty to agree with both of them, as a matter of social amenity, and make a present to them of the things men are fighting for. I would not make a present of the things men are fighting for to my best friend, or to my mother, or to God Himself. I yield when it is a question of local domestic politics. I yield when it is a question of the internal economy of a foreign nation. I will yield even when it is a question which to send first to China—vital war supplies or Coca-Cola for the American pilots in China. But I will not yield when it is a question of freedom, because I mean it, and I believe in it, and I know that we have today no alternative but to choose between empire and freedom. Because Churchill is so unashamedly for the principle of empire, I am sure he was a bad student of Greek at school. This does not matter; what really matters is that, by his domination of Allied war and peace aims, he is changing the character, the issues and the objectives of this war, in which Russian, Chinese, English and American boys have to pay with their lives. This is too important a matter to be hushed up even among true friends of England.

The fact is, no one has the right to make a present of the things men are fighting for to his best friend, or to his mother, or even to God. In every age and every period of history, after every war and every revolution, Liberty and Reaction go side by side together and struggle for supremacy for the moment. It is every man's duty to use his intelligence and stand by Liberty and the revolutionists, and fight the Old Guards of Reaction without fear and without favor. Some American editors wish to coddle both at the same time. But there stands the Old Guard, faithful unto death, taking an oath to preside over the nonliquidation of the British Empire. Despise not the Old Guard, American editors. There is much wisdom in his old head. Beware of the man who always finds God on his side. When the Old Guard announces that he "means to hold his

own," including what belongs inalienably to the Indians, and
the Chinese, Americans and Russians might just as well fight
for the British Empire, are we to say, "Amen"? It would be
perfectly satisfactory to me if this were a private war between
Germany and England. Let whoever wins hold his own, while
the subject nations are their pawns. If the subject nations do
not like it, that is matter for consideration in another separate
war between the "pawns" and their masters. But this is not a
private war, and other peoples are involved. When the British
Premier declares his intention to go on ruling the British possessions, the Chinese at once think of Hong Kong, the Indians
of India, the Dutch of Java, and the Americans of the Statue
of Liberty.

Prime Minister Winston Churchill, discussing the future
of the British Empire in the House of Commons, said on
March 17, 1943, "The government is convinced that the administration of British colonies must continue to be the sole
responsibility of Great Britain." This clearly, definitely, and unmistakably reveals that Churchill envisages the keeping of
India, Burma, the Malay States, the Straits Settlements, Hong
Kong, Ceylon, and other possessions. It also necessitates in fairness allowing other empires to keep theirs. The picture is,
therefore, definitely the restoration of white empires in Asia.
My view of Churchill as the Prince Metternich of the next
Peace Conference is therefore correct.

It is wrong to assume that Churchill forgets Asia; he never
forgets Asia—as a group of colonies. Perhaps what we are
liquidating is not the British Empire but the whole imperialist
system of a world half free and half slave. The question is
whether or not we are fighting for certain principles to make a
future war impossible and to make a juster and better world.
But these are obnoxious questions all—whether the liquidation
of the British Empire, or of the Dutch Empire, or the French,
or the Japanese Empire. Let's not talk about them. Win the
war first. When the war is over, Prince Metternich will surely

be there, and then the wrangle will begin. Then thirty or forty years later, we shall start all over again.

History cannot be understood through the inconsequential issues of details that newspapers so busily discuss, after they have been censored. History can be understood only as seen in the minds of men who direct a nation's policy. While Indians claim that Sir Stafford Cripps in the early stages of the discussion promised them a National "Cabinet," and Cripps' followers just as hotly deny he ever promised them so much real power as a National "Cabinet," only fools will deceive themselves that they have the real facts of the situation. Cripps' mission can be properly understood only by studying the mind of the modern Pericles who initiated and directed the whole Cripps' mission. Anyone who reads the following statements of Winston Churchill regarding his basic attitude toward India, in 1930-1931, and still cannot understand why Cripps failed must be something of a moron. In order to understand the handling of India, we must understand our Pericles. In January, 1930, Winston Churchill said, "Sooner or later you will have to crush Gandhi and the Indian Congress and all they stand for"—which happens to be the principles of the Atlantic Charter as applied to India. During the Simon Commission and after, he was the loudest in protesting against negotiating with the Indian leaders as injuring the prestige of the Empire and its public servants. In March, 1931, he said, ". . . We are assigning exaggerated importance to individuals in India with whom we shall never be able to agree and are injuring the prestige and strength of the British Government in India for dealing with all these problems." In February, 1931, he said, "To transfer that responsibility to this highly artificial and restricted oligarchy of Indian politicians would be a retrograde act. It would be a shameful act. It would be an act of cowardice, desertion and dishonor. It would bring upon Great Britain a moral shame which would challenge forever the reputation of the British Empire as a valiant and benignant force in

the history of mankind." This is Kiplingesque, both Churchill and Kipling having been press reporters of the Boer
War and sharing the same opinion about "the lesser breeds
without the law." Alas, in the sixteenth century, he might have
been heroic; in the seventeenth and the eighteenth, he might
have been competent; in the nineteenth, he might have been
great; but in the twentieth, he is a Kiplingesque anachronism.
His principles firm, his language clear, his purpose determined,
he has explained not only the Cripps' mission but the entire
India policy, present and future, in those words. Pericles could
not have spoken with greater dignity while his Empire flour-
ished, Cleon the leather merchant could not have been more
patriotic, Eucrates the rope-seller could not have been more
determined, and even Hyperbolus the lampmaker could not
have babbled in sweeter notes to Athenian ears. I may be excused if the lines of Matthew Arnold on "Dover Beach" come
irresistibly to my mind:

> Sophocles long ago,
> Heard it on the Aegean, and it brought
> Into his mind the turbid ebb and flow
> Of human misery; we
> Find also in the sound a thought,
> Hearing it by this distant northern sea.
>
> The sea of faith
> Was once, too, at the full, and round earth's shore
> Lay like the folds of a bright girdle furl'd.
> But now I only hear
> Its melancholy, long, withdrawing roar,
> Retreating, to the breath
> Of the night-wind, down the vast edges drear
> And naked shingles of the world.
>
> . . . .
>
> And we are here as on a darkling plain
> Swept with confused alarms of struggle and flight
> Where ignorant armies clash by night.

So we will not go into the issues of the India problem. Both the Hindus and the English have perfect arguments and, forgetting the central issue of human freedom, can confuse you with a mass of details. There is never a time when a person wants to do a thing and fails to find reasons for his action, or when a great nation decides upon an objective and fails to find the plausible procedure. Sometimes to enter into argument with a person is to pay him the compliment of believing in the worth of his arguments.

I am sure that if the Indians were told that there are Protestants and Catholics and Jews in the United States, and New Dealers and anti-New Dealers and Republicans and Democrats and Communists and Socialists and Yankees and Southerners and Negroes and Baptists and Methodists and Seventh Day Adventists and Episcopalians and Mormons, and that Jews, Italians, Greeks, and Irish live on the same streets in Jersey City, and that there are probably two hundred and fifty Christian sects in America, the Indians would despair of ever unraveling the racial and religious complexities of the United States. Yet Hindus and Moslems live on the same streets in India and get along just as well as, if not better than, the Italians and the Irish in Brooklyn. What is more important, they are all united upon one thing, the freedom of their country—unless it be two things, the freedom of their country and hatred of the English. The same would be true of the Croats and the Serbs and Jews and Catholics in Jugoslavia, which we did not hesitate to join together in one country when it suited our purpose. The fact is that if the Moslems did not exist, the English would have to invent them. Religion is the greatest godsend to the British Empire, and the English may well thank the gods for it. The British Empire and monotheism don't go together. Polytheism is more valuable than you think.

But I will, and I must, go into the issue of India as the issue of freedom for all peoples. Wearing no monocle, and unable to agree with Lady Astor, I happen to think of the freedom of

India exactly as I think of the freedom of Norway or Greece or Poland. I should be equally opposed to the extermination of freedom in Greece or Poland, either by Germany or by Russia, no matter what my sympathy for Russia and what my antipathy for Nazi Germany.

Now this attitude happens to be very difficult to understand. Some Americans can make the convenient difference between freedom from England for the Thirteen Colonies and freedom from England for India. Words spoken by Tom Paine are regarded as the Bible of Democracy; the same words spoken by Gandhi or Nehru are regarded as heresy and treason to our war effort. Not being an American, I cannot see the difference. To me, George Washington was as "anti-British" as Gandhi or Nehru, and just as stubborn. A binocular vision is an inconvenient thing. I know that Churchill is tremendously popular in New York, and I could have been a little smooth and applauded the hero I admired during Dunkirk. But I prefer to stick to my binoculars or to my two naked eyes.

I am dense enough not to be able to see the difference between the Indians fighting for their freedom and the French underground organization fighting for theirs. The Government of India has published a White Paper showing that the Congress leaders are guilty of actions or speeches leading to popular uprisings and sabotage. Two East India trunk railways were sabotaged, it is stated. If the Paris-Lille and Paris-Lyons Railways had been sabotaged, how the American press would have hailed those brave fighters for freedom and liberators of mankind! What tribute to the human spirit, evidence that it can never be conquered by physical force! Two trunk railways have been sabotaged in India and I agree this is highly regrettable because it hampers our war effort. But what would you have the Indians do?

For two and a half years after England had declared war on behalf of India without first consulting the Indians themselves, the Congress leaders held off, while the English would

do nothing to improve the situation. Frantic appeals for freedom and the immediate proximity of the Japanese in Burma
precipitated the Cripps' mission. The Indians wanted real power
in the defense of their country; the British Government would
not give it to them. The only solid accomplishment of the
Cripps' mission was that the idea of "Pakistan" received English official blessing and laid the basis for future dissensions in
India. Appeals for reopening negotiations after the Cripps' mission were vain. The war over India was fought in America;
the English had won here and were satisfied. The Congress
and Indian popular opinion were getting restive. Indian bitter-
ness mounted and Indian morale deteriorated. The English
rulers were still silent. What would you have the Indians do?
Address more prayers to stones?

After every effort to reopen negotiations had failed, Gandhi
gave advance notice to the Viceroy of India about the civil dis-
obedience campaign to be started. The English would not be
intimidated. Gandhi begged the Viceroy for a chance to see
him. The Viceroy with true viceregal dignity refused. The
Congress leaders were put in jail, illegally, according to English judges. The unarmed "rebellion" was quelled. The situation was "well in hand." The American press expressed the
opinion that after this success of force, the English would be
"magnanimous in victory," and some effort at reopening negotiations might be made. The English were still very "firm."

After waiting exactly six months, Gandhi announced his
intention to fast, as a protest against a moral wrong, not a personal wrong committed against himself, but a moral wrong
against his nation. He knew he was addressing a prayer to
stones, but he could not do otherwise. Acquit him or condemn
him, Gandhi would not alter his ways. Gandhi was stubborn
and the Viceroy was still adamant. Gandhi was in imminent
danger of death, and the last blow was about to be struck
against all hopes of future co-operation between England and
India. The Government of India published a seventy-six-page

White Paper, showing that the Congress was guilty of acts and thoughts leading to violence. It is the duty of the Government of India, we are told, to maintain peace and order, and the Congress leaders are disturbing it. "Anyway, we are getting as much from India by force as we could by any other method. Meanwhile, the situation is well in hand. And we are fighting for liberty."

The whole question of the correctness of the Karma doctrine depends on whether one believes the ripples of action stop there, like a closed chapter, or go on to join forces with other new ripples.

If what the British Government had wanted was a show of strength to uphold the Empire's prestige against a helpless subject nation, it got it. But if the British Government set out to regain the love of the Indian people and have better co-operation in the future, then they have lost their chance forever. Repression by force of rebellion, armed or unarmed, could be understood and even excused. But after the English demonstrated their superior physical force, and satisfied themselves and the world that they were still the master, the Congress leaders were still denied the opportunity of coming together with non-Congress leaders to work out a political solution, after an explicit request by the Indian leaders then out of jail (October, 1942). I cannot excuse this stupid English policy. The plea that "the Indians themselves would not come together" makes no sense to me. Separate detention cells are hardly the ideal situation for exchange of ideas, even among the Indian Yogi. And Gandhi is not a Yogi. "Thoughts that burst prison walls" is a fine literary flourish, but is not for mortal men like Rajagopalacharia or Sapru or Nehru.

The whole English policy makes sense to me only on the supposition, which is real, that what the Asiatics think or feel about it does not matter so long as the "Allies" have superior weapons. In fact, the whole conduct of the war in 1942 was psychologically determined by the one habit of thinking that what the Indians, the Chinese, and the Russians feel does not matter. Why? Because England and the United States are going to have an overwhelming air force.

The handling of the problem of India is merely a symptom of the failure to recognize the issue of freedom versus empire, of general spiritual unpreparedness and the belief that resentment, fear, and hatred do not matter so long as "the situation is well in hand," which simply means that rioters can be quelled by riot squads and which is exactly Hitler's way of thinking. We may be quite sure that after the war, the "situation" will be even better in hand, while the reasons for denying India freedom will remain just as valid. If the East and the West differ in political philosophy, it is usually in this: we disagree on the usefulness of temporary success achieved by arms. The Asiatic takes the more subtle view that *in the long run* good will or bad blood does count, that force is futile, and that there can be no peace until there is peace in the human heart (justice).

Today in this war, there is only one issue—Empire versus freedom. Two world leaders stand at the opposite poles: Chiang Kai-shek, for whom "patriotism is not enough," and Winston Churchill, for whom it is. Every thinking man must choose between the two. The measures and standards of European power politics and Asiatic ethical tradition do not meet. Mencius sharply defined them 2,200 years ago. "In a world of moral order, the great characters rule the small characters, and the great minds rule the small minds. In a world of moral chaos, the (physically) great rule the small, and the strong rule the weak. The (first) two are (the principles of) heaven. Those who obey Heaven shall survive, and those who disobey Heaven shall perish."

The issue of empire versus freedom is dividing us. While the war is on, we should hold the issues in abeyance to the extent of not letting them deter our common war efforts, even though our very strategy in Asia is determined by what we desire to see in Asia after the war. But it is the duty of every writer and thinker about contemporary trends to inform the public, to caution it if necessary, and in no case to falsify the picture of events. The seeds of disunity are already there, and since we cannot blink them away, we might as well point out their presence and forestall future dissensions before they become too advanced for remedy. If the war does not break us, the peace may. For it is absolutely certain that there will be no peace without collective security, and no collective security without American collaboration in the postwar world; but *America's collaboration or isolation will depend only on one thing, the character of the coming peace.* Sir Norman Angell goes about preaching about collective security and against American isolationism. But Sir Norman Angell has not the wit to see that all his preachings may be rendered vain by a peace treaty that provokes American revulsion. For more important than preaching about the importance of American collaboration is the securing of a peace that is worth American collaboration. Americans do not have to be preached to. Psychologically, present-day Americans are more ready to renounce isolationism than certain Europeans are ready to renounce the politics of power and imperialism. Both must be renounced at the same time; otherwise Europe is merely asking American collaboration in European imperialism.

I warn that American collaboration must ultimately depend on a just peace that the American people can approve, and that, however we may wish otherwise, an imperialistic peace will be followed by America's revulsion and reversion to isolation. Sir Norman Angell forgets how American isolationism arose as a matter of historical fact. It arose out of revulsion against the Versailles Treaty and out of a sad disillusion that the "war to end all wars" had turned out to be a war for spoils. If another Versailles comes, the American nation will feel such a revulsion against being the victim of wily European politics that they will withdraw in disillusionment and disgust again. Revulsion against and disgust with the crushing of ideals after the stupendous sacrifices are human, and the American nation cannot be asked to be inhuman. For if American collaboration and American participation in the World Police are wanted, they are wanted to defend the world order laid down by the coming peace treaty, and the American people must be convinced that that world order is worth defending. In a hypothetical case where that world order consists of the restoration of Asiatic colonies of the European powers, the function of the World Police will be to maintain by force that system of colonies, with American money and lives pledged to its maintenance. But America, like China, happens to be in a curious position; it has not got a single colony. Take away from the Americans certain principles of justice, and they will have nothing to fight for or worth fighting for.

I believe the principles of the Atlantic Charter are an adequate and dependable basis for a durable peace, even as President Wilson's Fourteen Points, if not sacrificed and scrapped at the time of peace negotiations, would have been an adequate and dependable basis for peace. Yet these very principles are already branded by one of the Charter's initiators as "fairy tales" and the discussion of their application at present is already regarded as "dangerous."

America's stand is clear. The cause in this war is the freedom of all peoples and all nations of the earth. The Atlantic Charter is meant to apply to all peoples "everywhere." The American people are with President Roosevelt. America's stand is clear. The flag of freedom has not been pulled halfway down.

Yet there is unfinished business between the two friends who drafted and signed the Atlantic Charter. Over a year has elapsed since President Roosevelt defined its scope and Winston Churchill will not say with Roosevelt that the Atlantic Charter applies to "all peoples everywhere." He has refused to define its scope or give assurance that the American interpretation is right. He refused its application to India by saying that the provisions of the Charter did not "qualify in any way the various statements of policy which have been made from time to time about the development of constitutional government in India, Burma, or other parts of the British Empire." In other words, the noble principles of the Atlantic Charter were for everybody to practice except the rulers of the British Empire. Note that his own "various statements" on the subject were, in December, 1931, "I did not contemplate India having the same constitutional rights and system as Canada *in any period which we can foresee*"; and in January, 1931, "No one has supposed that except in a purely ceremonial sense in the way in which representatives of India attended the conferences during the war, that *principle and policy for India would be carried into effect in any time which it is reasonable or useful for us to foresee.*"

But that was back in 1931. The Atlantic Charter was signed in the summer of 1941. America had not yet entered the war then. There was an advantage in leaving it undefined, for if Churchill had defined it then as he has now, America might never have entered a war for empire. But the Allies have had successes in 1942 and 1943, the prospects of victory are visible, England is growing confident and strong, and America has already irrevocably committed herself to the war. What he had left undefined he has now defined to a nicety. When, on March 17, 1943, J. McGovern, Laborite, asked whether the Churchill statement on the British Empire meant that "Britain does not intend to give up its occupied territories at the end of the war, as well as Germany," Churchill retorted, "That would be a very insulting parallel to draw." (Associated Press, according to the *New York Herald Tribune,* March 18, 1943). Lest he should be misunderstood as construing the Atlantic Charter to mean liberation of countries subjected by England as well as those subjected by Germany, he took special care to let the world know exactly what he meant through Brendan Bracken. If anyone "is going to make the catastrophic error of destroying or handing over our goodly heritage, I think there is enough toughness in the fibre of the empire to resist such a suggestion. . . . We must fight for our rights," he declared to Bracken. "Having been a foundation member of the United Nations, we are not going to tell our people they can be pushed around by any other nation in the world. It is the duty of the United Nations to remain united."

It is common sense to say that, even as the date for the independence of the Philippines has convinced the Filipinos of America's sincerity, so a date set for India's independence would convince the Indians of England's sincerity. Why then has the date not been set, and who opposed it? We read in John T. Whitaker's *We Cannot Escape History* the illuminating account. "A group in the cabinet decided to flush his [Churchill's] hand and force immediate action. As one of the men in that session later expressed it, 'Mr. Amery had finished his suggestion that we should promise India dominion status at a fixed period after the defeat of Hitler. Other members of the government were prepared to support his initiative. Before they could speak, Mr. Churchill let out a roar like a wounded lion. The room was cleared as swiftly as if there had been a lion among us in very truth. As yet the subject has not been raised again.'" (p. 243)

That is why we are confused. The issue of empire versus freedom cannot and may not be evaded, though Churchill took care to talk of "winning the war first" and evade it as best he could before the tide turned. He knows at least what he stands for, and says so, and President Roosevelt does not know what to do, or whether it would be the wise thing to contradict him now. So long as Roosevelt keeps silent on the issue of freedom versus empire and avoids a verbal tilt with his friend, the world must remain confused about our war aims. Know the Old Guard, and forget that he wears a bowler; in other times and in Austria, he might have worn a mustache. Forget that he is English, or that, as the *New York Times* described him ("Re-

view of the Week," March 28, 1943), he has been "for the past
two decades a Tory of Tories," or as Harold Callender said in
the same issue, that he is "a sincere imperialist of the romantic
Kipling era." The age has no use for imperialists of the romantic Kipling era, nor for Prince Metternichs.

That is why we are today already in confusion about the
applicability of the Atlantic Charter, which raises issues regarded by British Prime Minister Churchill as "dangerous" to
discuss now, according to the *New York Times* editorial of
April 4, 1943.

> Yet the issues have been raised [according to the same
> editorial], and out of the debate are emerging two broad
> concepts for an international organization for the future.
> One, based on a strict interpretation of the Atlantic Char-
> ter, envisages a world in which large and small nations
> will live side by side on terms of equality and cooperate
> politically and economically through some kind of world
> organization for purposes of collective security and mutual
> welfare. The other, more European-bound, envisages a
> Europe under the joint guardianship of Russia and Great
> Britain, with the smaller nations leaning on the one or the
> other of these two powers according to proximity. . . .
> *The first concept may be utopian, but it is the American
> idea expressed in global terms.* It is on this idea that Amer-
> ica deals with local authorities as it finds them, and still
> recognizes the integrity of the small Baltic states on Rus-
> sia's frontier. The second concept is not utopian, but re-
> alistically based on a balance of power and power politics.

The same editorial concludes with the profound remarks:

> Here we face a situation in which two considerations
> are implicit. *On the nature of the postwar settlements will
> depend in large degree America's final attitude toward in-*

ternational cooperation. At the same time, evidence or lack of evidence which we show now of our willingness to play an active part in world affairs, when the fighting ends, will be the most important single factor in shaping the character of the postwar treaties.

To be forewarned is to be forearmed. If American collaboration is wanted both during and after the war, there is a price for it, and that price may not be less than freedom of mankind and the principles of equality and justice. My observation is that the American nation is perfectly willing to pay the colossal price of world collaboration during and after the war if it can be convinced that it is worth the price. It is in this sense that indications of reversion to a spoils system of the Versailles pattern frighten me. There will be no collective security if some one nation wants only to collect and fails to recollect. It is in this sense that my heart sank within me when I read in the March, 1943, issue of *Britain,* the following statement by Sir Edward Grigg, condensed from his article in the *London Sunday Times:*

> Both the British and the American Governments have declared to France that her empire will be restored in its entirety, and to Spain and Portugal that no part of their empires will be taken from them. We must assume that similar assurance, if required, would be given to the two colonial powers which are members of the United Nations —Holland and Belgium. Is it, then, the British Colonial Empire only which is to go into liquidation?

Sir Edward Grigg was Governor of Kenya and has held other high offices in the British Government. Secret treaties like those preceding Versailles are already beginning. The character of the war is becoming clearer every day. Old dogs cannot learn new tricks and never will. This generation of political minds cannot learn to fight a new war and devise a new peace. That was how the Fourteen Points of Wilson were sacrificed, and that is how the principles of the Atlantic Charter are already placed in doubt and will be sacrificed later.

The Allies cannot win a common war with divided minds. Sooner or later, every man and woman must think and decide for himself or herself whether we are fighting for freedom or for empire, for between the two there is no compromise and besides the two there is no third alternative. We must choose between Roosevelt and Churchill, for we may not choose both. They are only two ideas.

6

WORLD WAR III

WHILE we consider binding up the economic sores of the postwar international society, we are not even beginning to scratch the surface of the moral malignant tumor that is called twentieth-century culture. The region of the tumor being sensitive, our statesmen and publicists are too scared to touch its surface. That is why our governments have consistently followed the policy of "win the war first." For the time being, the win-the-war-first boys are having their way. The roots of all war—balance of power, domination by power, trade, and racial discrimination—are all there; not a single factor is lacking. All the lessons we could have taken from the Greek world are being ignored; all the sources of possible conflict, so plain now to the student of history, seem not to exist for the average planner of peace for the postwar world. The house built on sand by our learned architects will one day collapse.

For I have said that it is too late now to strangle Russia and China. England, America, Russia, and China will unquestionably be the powers that will determine the movements of history in the next half-century. According to the English, who are talking of giving India freedom after the war, there will be also the good will or hostility of another 400,000,000 people in Asia to reckon with. On the present pattern of Anglo-American domination of the war, which means definitely Anglo-American domination of the peace, we are clearly going back to the centuries-old European theory of balance of power. (We may, for purposes of the discussion, call the Anglo-American pattern of domination the "A-A" pattern.) The A-A pattern will devise "checks and balances" so that the A-A world and the non-A-A world will live in a kind of armed friendship and hostile cordiality. Different grades and formulas of "world-co-operation" or "world police force" will be put forth and orators will speak about the new era of good will and co-operation. Since power, however, is by definition something dynamic and not static, there is no such thing as an actual "balance of power." Some powers grow and others weaken during a period; some alliances deteriorate, new ones are formed. Then the balance is upset once more and the nations of the world are plunged once more into bloodshed until a new "balance" is devised by a new generation of peace architects using the old squares and compasses. The balance of power theory has kept Europe in periodic bloodshed every thirty or forty years for the last few centuries. The transference of the tactics of power politics to the world as a whole can only mean the transformation of this earth into a periodic arena. Power politics and the balance of power always set up a state of tension among the states, very similar to walking on a tight rope. This state produces a condition of mutual fears and suspicions, and as some of the states grow in power, the fears and suspicions grow. For ten years preceding World War I and World War II, one could see this mounting tension and fear and insecurity, until someone decided it was time to strike first. The same state of fears and antagonisms will inevitably produce the same result. The pattern is unchangeable.

Thus World War III will come. The ferocity of future wars will not deter us, the magnitude of sacrifice will not daunt us, nor will the cries of mothers and wives keep us from the path of duty, for young men of another generation, without the experience of this war, will go forth to save civilization and die for six, seven, or perhaps eight freedoms. But the blood that will be shed all over the globe will make our present sacrifices look like grandmothers' nightmares. Nature is a spendthrift in birth and in slaughter. If men are ready for a big-scale fratricide, God is ready, too. In half a million years, God can create a bigger, better, and more reasonable species of beings. Nor will those who believe in power politics have the right to complain. Since power politicians defend their course of action on naturalism or the natural "struggle for power," they must also be ready to accept its consequences. If they pride themselves on their "realism" about politics and war, they must also be "realistic" about the consequences of war.

Nor can we be scared now by the appearance of comets and strange stars. Gabriel will not descend on the earthly plains and speak to the sons of men. Harmless miracles of changing water into wine will not stand our scientific scrutiny. A Jonah spat out from a whale will not deceive us, but after careful questioning by reporters will be confined to an insane asylum. William James's voice will not come from the dead to assure us of a future life. The heavens will not rain fire and brimstone, and there will be neither a pillar of a cloud to lead us by day, nor a pillar of fire to light us by night. Neither praying, nor fasting, nor the singing of psalms, nor the burning of candles will avail. For us, at least, it will be a God-empty world. There will be just nothing to do about it.

No diplomat of course will talk of anything but good will and the friendship of nations, and no diplomat will be fool enough to act on these protestations. All forms of mandates, tariff problems, and police zones and international air bases will be discussed and in time worked out. They may even write a Fifty Years' Peace, which will be worth as much as the Fifty Years' Peace of Nicias. All the peace delegates will be good men, too, for they will be men who go to church; they will be men of culture and learning and experience, good fathers, good husbands, and good patriots all. But they will build a house on sand.

Since the A-A school of thought is a very real, very potent, and very influential one at present, the consequences of such a policy of armed friendship against the non-English-speaking world are fairly predictable. How well the A-A group can divide the non-A-A group will depend largely upon the astuteness of their statesmanship. China is pledged to A-A cooperation in her foreign policy at present. How well that armed friendship will materialize will depend on how successfully the United States and England will drive China into the lap of Russia. This, in turn, depends on China's judgment as to what kind of allies will be more dependable and sincere in the next war, and this again depends on her experiences with her allies in the present war and the ensuing peace settlement. China's position is decidedly anomalous, with regard to racial and imperialist groupings though not with regard to ideology. Being herself a nonindustrialized and therefore nonimperialist nation, the possibility of her reaching a basis of equal partnership with imperialist nations has never been proved or studied carefully. But certain it is that she will not stand for social "snubbing" for long, and she may give up trying to "keep up with the Joneses" and look about for more heavily pigmented allies and friends. Such a contingency would be indeed tragic for the whole world, particularly with the background of Indian hostility against the English being fanned into a living flame right now. Again, we shall not escape history.

It should be noted also that long before such a conflict comes to pass, the antagonism of rising forces will be the logical situation for the resurgence of Japan and Germany. Both sides will secretly bid for their support and encourage them to re-arm, as we did so successfully in the 1930-1940 decade. In other words, in spite of all our sacrifices during this war, we shall start all over again. That men should die is hard enough for the mothers of men; that they should die in vain is heart-breaking.

I may be wrong in prognostications of particular trends and phases of development. But some such thinking and heart-searching along historic lines on the subject of growth, balance, and unbalancing of power are needed. The adequacy of power politics as a principle must be called into question; the de-pendability of the cardinal principle of balance of power in building a stable peace must be debated, talked about, and chal-lenged. Only so can there be depth in our reasoning. *The changes in our way of thinking must be basic if we are to be saved.*

There is a pattern of things invisible, of karmatic currents in human history, that can be seen only with the eyes of the mind. Sometimes it is given to poets to foretell the future, not by astrology, but by acquaintance with the laws of the spirit. To such extraordinary minds, these laws become so vivid that they assume the character of a "vision." Heinrich Heine was such a poet with such an uncanny vision. From an intimate and intuitive knowledge of the German mind, he could proph-esy the "German Revolution" and the character of the present-day Nazi spirit with a frightening accuracy, and from a knowledge of the forces developing in European thought, he could prophesy the "European or World Revolution" and pre-dict with striking clairvoyant power certain phases unrolling before our eyes today. Speaking of the German thunder, com-ing slowly but surely, he said:

Then, when you hear the rumble and clatter—beware, Frenchmen, you neighbors' children. . . . Don't smile at my advice, the advice of a dreamer who warns you of Kantians, Fichteans, and natural philosophers. *Don't smile at the visionary who expects the same revolution in the material world which has taken place in the realm of the spirit.*

Writing in 1834, in *Religion and Philosophy in Germany,* Heine spoke of the breaking of the brittle talisman, the Christian Cross, and the resurgence of the gods of the German forests and warned that we should hear a "crash as nothing ever crashed in world history."

The German revolution will not be milder and gentler because it was preceded by Kant's *Critique,* by Fichte's transcendental idealism, and even by the philosophy of nature. . . . For if the Kantian's hand strikes strongly because his heart is moved by no traditional respect—if the Fichtean courageously defies all danger because for him it does not really exist—the philosopher of nature will be fearful because he can join the primeval forces of nature, because he can call up the demoniac energies of ancient Germanic pantheism, and because then there will awake in him that fighting folly that we find among the ancient Germans, that fights neither to kill nor to conquer, but simply to fight. Christianity has—and that is its fairest merit—somewhat mitigated that brutal German lust for battle. But it could not destroy it; and once the taming talisman, the Cross, is broken, the savagery of the old battlers will flare up again, the insane rage of which Nordic bards have so much to say and sing. That talisman is brittle. The day will come when it will pitiably collapse. Then the old stone gods will rise from forgotten rubble and rub the dust of a thousand years from their eyes; and Thor will leap up and with his giant hammer start smashing Gothic cathedrals. . . .

. . . and when you hear a crash as nothing ever crashed in world history, you'll know that the German thunder has hit the mark. At that sound the eagles will fall dead from the sky and the lions in the farthest desert of Africa will pull in their tails and slink away into their royal caves. A play will be performed that will make the French Revolution seem like a harmless idyll in comparison. . . .

Beware! I wish you well; that is why I tell you the bitter truth. You have more to fear from a liberated Germany than from the whole Holy Alliance with all its Croats and Cossacks . . .[11]

One hundred and one years ago, in 1842, he prophesied the "World Revolution," a drama of which we have seen the beginning and he could not tell the end. He, the friend of Karl Marx, saw the character of revolutionary thought, but he also, with his poet's vision, foresaw the course of the present war and the fate of Germany, France, England, and Russia in this war all too clearly:

Communism is the secret name of the dread antagonist setting proletarian rule with all its consequences against the present bourgeois regime. It will be a frightful duel. How will it end? No one knows but gods and goddesses acquainted with the future. We only know this much: Communism, though little discussed now and loitering in hidden garrets on miserable straw pallets, is the dark hero destined for a great, if temporary, role in the modern tragedy. . . .

It would be war, the ghastliest war of destruction—which would unfortunately call the two noblest nations of civilization into the arena, to the ruin of both: France and Germany. England, the great sea serpent always able to crawl back into its vast watery lair, and Russia, which also

[11] *Heinrich Heine: Works of Prose*, ed. by Hermann Kesten, pp. 51-53.

has the safest hiding places in its vast fir forests, steppes and icy wastes—those two, in a normal political war, cannot be annihilated even by the most crushing defeats. But Germany is far more menaced in such cases, and France in particular could lose her political existence in the most pitiful manner.

That, however, would only be the first act of the great melodrama, the prologue, as it were. The second act is the European and the World Revolution, the great duel between the destitute and the aristocracy of wealth; and in that there will be no mention of either nationality or religion: there will be only one fatherland, the globe, and only one faith, that in happiness on earth. Will the religious doctrines of the past rise in all countries, in desperate resistance—and will perhaps this attempt constitute the third act? Will the old absolutist tradition reenter the stage, though in a new costume and with new cues and slogans? How could that drama end?

I do not know; but I think that eventually the great sea serpent will have its head crushed, and the skin of the Northern bear will be pulled over his ears. There may be only one flock then and one shepherd—one free shepherd with an iron staff, and a shorn-alike, bleating-alike human herd!

Wild, gloomy times are roaring toward us, and a prophet wishing to write a new apocalypse would have to invent entirely new beasts—beasts so terrible that St. John's older animal symbols would be like gentle doves and cupids in comparison. The gods are veiling their faces in pity on the children of man, their long-time charges, and perhaps over their own fate. The future smells of Russian leather, blood, godlessness, and many whippings. I should advise our grandchildren to be born with very thick skins on their backs." [12]

---

[12] *Ibid.*, pp. 136-138.

Only to poets are the shapes of things to come so clear. He knew the German spirit through and through, and he knew the progress of the human spirit in Europe through and through. Alas, that he had lived also through an age of revolution and disillusionment, of the revolutions and Prince Metternich! That was why he cried, "Beware! I wish you well; that is why I tell you the bitter truth." Because he saw the "revolution in the realm of the spirit," he could also foretell the "same revolution in the material world."

We might yet try to see the further revolution in the realm of the spirit in the century after Heine, with far clearer indications of the direction in which it has been developing. We, too, might try to understand the character of the age we are living in, and grapple with the problem of moral decay and regeneration, although there is little evidence of regeneration and a great deal of decay. We, too, might be able to predict a disaster, but, once freed from the shackles of determinism, the wisest prophet would be the one who refused to predict.

II. THE METHOD

7

THE "WHITE MAN'S BURDEN"

THESE are indeed times that try men's souls. Effective planning of peace without a philosophy of peace is impossible. A revolution in thinking and in the method of thinking, of political events in particular and of human affairs in general, must be brought about before a revolution in world politics is possible. The standards of morality, particularly of international morality, in this decade are notoriously at a low ebb.

Compared with the French encyclopedists of the eighteenth century, we are unworthy progeny of our ancestors of that period of "Enlightenment." For fully equipped as we are with a philosophy of war, the psychology of war, the politics of war, and the implements of war, how can we escape war? The most important question now is: after all the bloodshed and sacrifice, shall we let it start all over again?

Ultimately, the problems of peace and war are determined by the character of the effective faiths of an age. The problems of peace are problems of man and the nature of man. I believe they are strictly philosophical problems, problems of the things that men believe in and live by. As I shall show later, it is ultimately a problem of determinism versus free will, of determinism of brute force and spiritual faith. Peace on earth is an act of faith, and without faith we shall not be saved. It happens that we are a generation without faith.

What we need above all is a theory of the rhythm of life and of the unity and interrelatedness of all things. Without that faith, the doctrine of force cannot be destroyed. The dichotomy between ideals and action must be resolved, and an all-inclusive, comprehensive philosophy must be produced whereby ideals may be brought down from the clouds again to activate the affairs of men on earth. High-flown idealism and pedestrian realism must be joined together, so that idealists are no longer regarded by businessmen as impractical and "realism" is no longer an excuse for dispensing with ideals in men's plans for action. The rhythm of life and the unity and interrelatedness of all things must be shown and shown conclusively, so that they become a part of our faith for daily action.

This will come about in the form of a spiritual softening of western philosophy, mental mellowness and moral maturity, a ripening of the sparkling wine of western intellect. There will be an inevitable maturing of the mind of this hard-hitting, competing, caustic, corrosive age, where the hardness of steel has entered into men's hearts and the iron of hate has corroded men's souls. In this Steel Age, it is not only that men's ships are made of steel plates; men's minds are also shaped thereby. "Nature is soft," says Laotse, but men's minds are hard. The human heart is one of the most changeful, elastic, flexible organs in nature; that is why it must not be tampered with.

> Be careful [says Laotse] not to interfere with the natural goodness of the heart of man. Man's heart may be forced down or stirred up. In each case the issue is fatal. By gentleness, the hardest heart may be softened. But try to cut and polish it, and it will glow like fire or freeze like ice. In the twinkling of an eye it will pass beyond the limits of the Four Seas. In repose, it is profoundly still; in motion, it flies up to the sky. Like an unruly horse, it cannot be held in check. Such is the human heart.

I have every reason to believe that the human heart is a runaway horse now.

What surprises me most in western thought is the almost complete absence of a philosophy of peace, by which I mean of peace, not merely as a hope in some utopian future, but peace as a normal condition of living in the present, as applied to the home, the nation, and the world. For instance, the technique of peaceful living, of domestic peace, national peace, and world peace, is hardly ever developed. Western social thought is either economics or political science. To me it is less satisfying than eating a juicy apple.

The technique of peace in the social and political sciences is either the equal distribution of goods, the balance of production and consumption and of import and export, or checks and balances, or the regalia of courts of justice and the rights and obligations arising out of scraps of paper, sworn to and notarized according to the due process of law. Society is conceived as an agglomeration of heterogeneous and conflicting interests brought to live at peace with one another by the mechanism of law courts which operate to eliminate excesses of liberty; in more liberal quarters, this concept is softened and extended to include moral restraint, or the restraint of the un-written law and public sentiment, with which Confucianism entirely agrees. In general, however, the western view of society and politics is legalistic and mathematical, like the point ra-tion coupons. Apart from the generous motivating forces of religion, the legal concept of a man living within the law is hardly a flattering theory of human life, in which the bachelor banker becomes the ideal citizen because as a banker he suc-cessfully dodges the taxes and as a bachelor he successfully dodges the women.

But even more than legalistic, the western view of the na-ture, function, and aim of human life is almost 95 per cent eco-nomic. It has gradually changed throughout the nineteenth and the twentieth centuries through the steady increase of inventions, so much that human progress itself has been already identified with rising standards of living. It is almost the whole of what we are talking, writing, and dreaming about.

From my college days, I have heard of the "white man's burden" and have often wondered what is inside that knapsack which the white man carries on his back around the globe. I have now discovered that it is only canned goods. Poor Kipling, he would not have remained alive and returned to be Lord Rector of St. Andrews if he were deprived during his stay in India of his store of corned beef and sardines. Still you cannot deny that he successfully converted corned beef and sardines into some good rousing verse, breathing pluck and faith in a so very enlightened scheme of shipping that made corned beef obtainable in far away Allahabad and Lahore.

The charge of "materialism" is no mere *cliché*. Materialism is the very stuff and fiber of modern thinking, which domi-nates all postwar planning and makes a philosophy of peace impossible. Is it not true that almost all our proposals for the future peace stem from the one assumption that the cure for the ills of economic progress is more economic progress? Are we not thinking of peace merely in terms of a free exchange of trade, free flow of material, and "prosperity"? In other words, peace is canned goods, bigger and better canned goods. Peace is a condition where we may sell and sell abundantly. "Heaven" itself is a concrete, fire-proof warehouse stocked to the ceiling with canned goods. For the world is now business, political business and economic business. A nation is a concern, a government is only its shop counter, and its diplomats are its traveling salesmen trying to outsell its competitors and beat them to a new market, and its publicists and thinkers are its expert accountants. The audacity of these thinkers of peace hurts my soul.

Who can deny that economic thinking has superseded all other forms of thinking, that economic issues have obscured all other issues, that we are thinking of nothing but applying poultices to our economic sores, and that our highest spiritual hope is good business and plenty of consumer goods for all? And who can deny that this power and profit motive contains in itself the seeds of future wars? Who can gainsay the fact that we are living in a decade of moral and spiritual bankruptcy and of the elimination of morals from politics? Far from being an empty phrase, materialism colors 95 per cent of our effective thinking. In fact, it is strangling our thinking.

Soap is good. That is taken for granted. Nothing impresses me more in American civilization than the fact that soap here is good and cheap and available to all. At American hotels, it is as costless as fresh air. Washing is both convenient and pleasant in the United States. Americans are hardly aware of it, but Europeans and Orientals are when they come to visit America. Almost any soap you buy is bound to be of high quality. It is not an article of luxury; soap with the most exquisite perfume is obtainable even at the five-and-ten-cent stores. Soap has become democratic. At least one problem has been solved. The problem of removing stains from dresses and rugs and scratches from varnished tables, too, has been solved ably; there exist almost miraculous remedies.

Technological progress and industrial research have gathered such momentum that nothing is going to stop them. Imprison all the scientists and disgrace all the directors of Du Pont and General Electric, and material progress will still go on. Condemn the inventors of fluorescent paint and disfranchise the perfectors of the air-cooling system, and new inventors will rise from the Arizona desert and be shipped by some underground organization to New York and Detroit with the connivance of the police. You cannot dethrone science and you need not.

Soap is plentiful. That is a positive achievement of American democracy. The striking thing is that there is at the same time a complete absence of a philosophy of peace. To give soap to Hottentots, while American soap-makers at home make more money, is not the road to peace. But that is the highest intellectual level we can rise to. On the proposed utopian plan to sell soap to four hundred million Indians there is always complete agreement, and even some degree of enthusiasm. On the proposal to give India freedom, there are many reservations, hesitations, rationalizations, and beating about the bush, and not a trace of enthusiasm. If the Allies ever give back India's freedom, it will be with a feeling of "just-too-bad, there's-nothing-else-you-can-do" despondency. Under such circumstances, it is easy to be a spiritual prophet and denounce like Savonarola the materialism of this age. It is no distinction at all. Just some common sense will enable anyone to see this point. The strange thing is, common sense is so uncommon. We have been awed into silence by the economist, all of us. That is all.

If there is one thing I can be sadistic about, it is swine-and-slop Economics. My only desire in life is to see the Economist, the law-giver of Europe, dethroned, disgraced, and hanged. I burn with rage whenever I see tables of percentages. If he were not so smug with his little facts, it would not arouse such a resentment in me. It's that expression which we see on the face of Ph.D. candidates—a stilted and hypnotized expression, doped with facts and figures and statistical averages and mechanical laws—a case of complete auto-intoxication. The impostor at least has a sense of humor, but the Economist is utterly humorless and sincere. He has a fear of emotions; all his educational training leads up to it. He wants to be objective only and prays God that he be delivered from all emotion. He knows, and knows for certain, that for 1937 it (never mind what) is $27\frac{1}{2}$ per cent, but for 1938, it is $34\frac{5}{8}$ per cent, and he is as proud of his fractions as a cobbler is proud of leather. A cobbler of Gotham, I was told, proposed to defend the city with leather. The Economist wants to defend the whole modern civilization with his fractions and statistical averages. Somehow if only the figures are juggled right, there will be peace in the world. He tells you, this is science; it is positive, objective knowledge. He has a special technique and a set of paraphernalia, with which he overawes the outsiders, and a special language—what a language! It is his oracles, and the god he consults is Materialism, and of that god he is the high priest.

Peace, we are told, is a highly technical matter, like the making of synthetic rubber. It consists, we are told, of lowering tariff barriers, establishing international air routes and air bases, shipping and insurance credits and guarantee of capital investments abroad, easing of population pressures, raising the standard of living. Peace is just distributing ration coupons to the world. So if we get together an army of tariff experts, air experts, shipping experts, insurance experts, rubber experts, and cactus experts (of which there are fifty-seven varieties) and alfalfa experts (those who specialize in the crinkly alfalfa and the flat-leaf one), and divide all these experts into departments and sections, then we are going to have peace.

It is this form of materialism that is driving me mad. I have no wish to be a spiritual prophet, but the Fact-Cult has gone a little too far. The first step of wisdom is the realization of this folly—of the inadequacy of our conception of peace.

8

"GOVERNMENT BY MUSIC"

BUT what is a philosophy of peace? Peace is an ever-present condition of living, rather than the abstract condition to be devoutly wished for in some distant utopia. Peace is normal, as health is normal. We have to have a philosophy in which we believe that peace is positive and not merely the absence of conflicts and wars—a negative ideal. Peace is rich, peace is satisfying, peace is growth and movement and action and life. Peace is as natural as harmony because it is the normal way of man; man rejects war as he intuitively rejects discord or dissonance in music. And the psychology of domestic peace, national peace, and world peace cannot be very different—it is merely the harmony of social relationships. For that harmony of social relationships there is a technique. Human philosophy should occupy itself exclusively with that technique of social harmony.

Naturally, I have been searching in Chinese thought for elements that might be contributions to the philosophy of world peace. Human society in China is on the whole no better than human society in the West. There are squalor, poverty, quarrels, corruption, selfishness, and social injustice. There are as many reactionaries in China as in the West, only a little less appeasers in high places. The thought causes a shudder. After all, the man who deals with Darlan must envy Laval, who can deal directly with Hitler. Both proceed on the principle of expediency at the sacrifice of principles, but after all the man

who deals with an accessory must envy the man who is able
to deal with the principal. Man in China acts both on "principle" (*ching*) and on "expediency" (*ch'üan*), both fully recognized by Confucian teachers. But somehow he still believes in
moral principles and values and their validity in practical
action.

Where China utterly differs from the West are the three
contempts: the contempt for the soldier, the contempt for the
the police, and the contempt for lawyers. China has lived for
4,000 years without police and lawyers, and the soldier is de-
spised. It is an unmathematical way of life, arising from contempt for the mathematical way of thinking.

Evidently, here is a new approach. The Chinese believe
that when there are too many policemen, there can be no individual liberty, when there are too many lawyers, there can
be no justice, and when there are too many soldiers, there can
be no peace. Peace can be obtained only by putting the government in reverse. Since this is a world of mixed characters, let
there be a government to put a few fellows in jail. That is
all the government exists for. True justice is obtained by settlement out of court, and true peace is obtained when soldiers
are unseen, unheard of, and unknown. Ultimately the problem
of peace is the problem of general education in good manners
and music.

I am not joking when I say that this is the basic teaching
of Confucianism. It is the central, basic, and fundamental
teaching of Confucian philosophy, which merges political and
moral problems into one. For this is the strangest outcome of
the reputed Confucian good sense—government by good manners and by music. Americans, who are intensely practical, may
agree that government by police, particularly secret police, is
highly repellent. They may agree that government by law,
though workable, may be slightly inadequate and fall short
of the highest ideal. They know that government by a series of
verbotens in the Prussian style is not good enough for the dem-

ocratic individual, and that the good life is something more than obeying a series of "Thou shalt not's." They know that in a mature, full-grown democracy, peace and order ultimately depend on the decency and self-respect of the individual.

I like Americans best when I see them breaking laws and regulations, when I see at a movie theater that the audience's sympathy is with the stowaway and not with the law-upholding captain, and when I see on the trains between Washington and New York people smoking in every car marked "No Smoking." These are born democrats, I say. When the situation gets bad enough, it is not the Herr Conductor that will stop it, but the public, by somebody writing to the *New York Times* pleading against the danger of ashes burning babies' arms. If the public does not mind, neither will the American conductor. But imagine a Prussian crowd smoking in a car where smoking is *verboten!* They just can't do it, and that is why the Weimar Republic fell and the *Frankfurter Zeitung* turned tail and they needed a Hitler. Put a Hitler over an American crowd to tell them not to do this and not to do that, and see the result. He would not survive three months before his head was smashed. Democracy's reply to Prohibition was the speakeasies. The history of the speakeasies is the glorious history of exactly how much the American people would stand for *verbotens,* and of how they would obey even laws passed by themselves! I take off my hats to these Americans, because they are like my own people, the Chinese. You can't "prohibit" the Americans, nor can you the Chinese. An official prohibition to do a thing is an invitation to a Chinese to do it. Long live the identity of our causes!

Even so, the practical Americans must doubt Confucius' reputation for common sense when they hear of his proposal to govern a country by music. Only a Saroyan could have said a thing like that. Nevertheless, I maintain that Confucius was quite sane, as I shall try to show. Confucius actually "sang in

the rain." [13] Confucius did say it, and said it time and again all
his life. Such was his precept about government and his emphasis on worship and song that one of his disciples took his
words literally. When Confucius one day approached a city
where his disciple, Tseyu, had been made magistrate, he heard
public singing going on in the squares.

> Confucius grinned and said to Tseyu, "You are killing
> a chicken with a big cleaver for killing a cow." "But I
> heard from you," replied Tseyu, "that when the superior
> man had learned culture, he would become kind and when
> the common man learned culture, he would become self-
> disciplined." Confucius turned to the other disciples and
> said, "You fellows, what he says is right. I was only pull-
> ing his leg!" [14]

I have chosen this aspect of Confucianism to show, by way
of contrast, the Confucian emphasis on spiritual values, and to
reveal the devastating inadequacy of the economic solution for
peace. The adolescent idea that peace can be achieved by a
mechanical distribution of goods, its crudity and its inadequacy, will become apparent. We must soon come to the position of admitting that the man who talks of music and spiritual
harmony is not just a moron, and refuse to believe that only
the man who talks of canned goods is "practical." If practical
good sense means preoccupation with material realities of food
and clothing and shelter, that decidedly is not a characteristic
of Confucianism.

Of the factors of government, Confucius had this to say:

> Tsekung asked about government, and Confucius re-
> plied, "People must have sufficient to eat; there must be a
> sufficient army; and there must be faith in the nation."

---

[13] See the piece "Confucius Singing in the Rain," *With Love and Irony*, p. 167.
[14] *The Wisdom of China and India*, pp. 821-822.

"If you were forced to give up one of these three factors, what would you go without?" asked Tsekung. Confucius said, "I would go without the army first." "And if you were forced to go. without one of the two remaining factors, which would you rather go without?" asked Tsekung again. "I would go without sufficient food. *There have always been deaths in every generation, but a nation without faith cannot stand.*" [15]

Since the psychology of peace is the same, whether it be domestic, national, or world peace, the factors of such a peace, according to Confucius, may be appropriately examined here. We have been used to treating politics as a separate problem, as strictly a problem of the machinery of administration, cut apart from morals. Confucianism envisages the government as only one of the four factors of bringing about social order, "rituals, music, punishments and administration"; in fact, it is always contemptuous of a purely political solution as such. Only so can we understand the fantastic theory of government by music. The conception of peace is more than the mechanics of keeping good men out of jail and bad men in it; it is related to true manhood and to social and national health, in which music seems the best and most natural fruition of culture. It almost seems that the enjoyment of music provides the aim and end and *raison d'être* of culture itself.

For so are the nature and function of government and the nature of domestic, national, and world peace conceived:

It follows, therefore, that to govern a country without *li* (rituals, and the principle of moral order) is like tilling a field without a plough. To observe *li* without basing it on the standard of right is like tilling the field and forgetting to sow the seeds. To try to do right without cultivating knowledge is like sowing the seeds without weeding the

[15] *Ibid.*, p. 839.

field. To cultivate knowledge without bringing it back to the aim of true manhood is like weeding the field without harvesting it. And to arrive at the aim of true manhood without coming *to enjoy it through music* is like harvesting and forgetting to eat the harvest. To enjoy true manhood through music and not arrive at complete harmony with nature is like eating and not becoming well fed, or healthy.

When the four limbs are well developed and the skin is clear and the flesh is full, that is the health of the body. When the parents and children are affectionate, the brothers are good towards one another and the husband and wife live in harmony, that is the health of the family. When the higher officials obey the law and the lower officials are honest, the officers have regulated and well-defined functions and the king and ministers help one another on the right course, that is the health of the nation. When the Emperor rides in the carriage of Virtue, *with Music as his driver,* when the different rulers meet one another with courtesy, the officials regulate one another with law, the scholars urge one another by the standard of honesty, and the people are united in peace, that is the health of the world. This is called the Grand Harmony (*tashun*).[16]

From such a picture of world peace as the Grand Harmony, it is clear that peace is not the absence of conflicts, but the healthy result of a number of cultural forces. It is easy to understand therefore why a political solution is necessarily inadequate and shallow in the "governing" of a country. Government is more than governing—hence the role of rituals and music. The four factors of social order work for a common goal. "Li *(rituals), music, punishments and administration have*

---

[16] For this and the following quotations, see *Wisdom of Confucius* (Modern Library), pp. 239-240, and 252-261.

a common goal, which is to bring about unity in the people's hearts, and carry out the principles of political order."

The defense of government by music in *Liki* (chapter "On Music") is made in curiously psychological terms. Rituals and music help to achieve this social harmony by establishing the right likes and dislikes, or what we call good taste in the people. Social and political chaos comes from certain unregulated desires. Ultimately, there can be peace only when there is peace in the human heart; it cannot be imposed from without. These psychological facts showing the origins of world chaos are still true today:

> The nature of man is usually quiet, but when it is affected by the external world, it begins to have desires. With the thinking mind becoming conscious of the impact of the material world, we begin to have likes and dislikes. When the likes and dislikes are not properly controlled and our conscious minds are distracted by the material world, we lose our true selves and the principle of Reason in nature is destroyed. When man is constantly exposed to the things of the material world which affect him and does not control his likes and dislikes, then he is overwhelmed by the material reality and becomes dehumanized or materialistic. When man becomes dehumanized or materialistic then the principle of Reason in nature is destroyed and man is submerged in his own desires. From this arise rebellion, disobedience, cunning and deceit, and general immorality. We have then a picture of the strong bullying the weak, the majority persecuting the minority, the physically brave going for violence, the sick and crippled not being taken care of, and the aged and the young and helpless not cared for. This is the way of chaos.

The people are therefore controlled through the rituals and music instituted by the ancient kings . . . the rituals regulate the people's feelings; music establishes harmony in the sounds of the country; the administration orders their conduct and the punishments prevent crimes. *When rituals, music, punishments and administration are all in order, the principles of political order are complete.*

We are now in a position to follow the close connection between music and rituals and good government—a good government based on *good taste.*

Music unites, while rituals differentiate. Through union, the people come to be friendly toward one another, and through differentiation, the people come to learn respect for one another. If music predominates, the social structure becomes too amorphous, and if rituals predominate, social life becomes too rigid. To bring the people's inner feeling and external conduct into balance is the work of rituals and music. The establishment of rituals gives a well-defined sense of order and discipline, while the general spread of music and song establishes the general atmosphere of peace among the people. When good taste is distinguished from bad taste, then we have the means of distinguishing the good from the bad people, and when violence is prevented by the criminal law and the good men are selected for office, then the government becomes stable and orderly. With the doctrine of love for teaching affection, and the doctrine of duty for teaching moral rectitude, the people will then have learned to live in a moral order.

Music comes from the inside, while rituals come from the outside. Because music comes from the inside, it is characterized by quiet and calm. And because rituals come from the outside, they are characterized by formalism. Truly great music is always simple in movement, and truly great rituals are always simple in form. When good music prevails, there is no feeling of dissatisfaction, and when proper rituals prevail, there is no strife and struggle. When we say that by mere bowing in salute the king can rule the world, we mean thereby the influence of rituals and music. When the violent elements of a nation are kept quiet, the different rulers come to pay homage, the military weapons are locked up, the five classes of punishments are not brought into use, and the people have no worries and the Emperor has no anger, *then truly music has prevailed*. When the parents and children are affectionate toward one another, the juniors respect the elders, and this respect is extended to all people in the country, and the Emperor himself lives such an exemplary life, *then we may truly say that* li *has prevailed."*

The constant contrasts of rituals and music as instruments of social and political order are philosophic and quite revealing and must help to correct the impression that practical Confucianism deals only with kitchen pots and pans, or can ever descend to the level of economic thought which reduces civilization and progress to the two questions of alimentation ("a quart of milk") and elimination (the flush toilet). "Truly great music shares the principle of harmony with the universe, and truly great ritualism shares the principle of distinctions with the universe." Again, "Music expresses the harmony of the universe, while rituals express the order of the universe. Through harmony all things are influenced, and through order all things have their proper place." Or again, "Music illustrates the primordial forces of nature, while rituals reflect the products of the creation. Heaven represents the principle of motion, while Earth represents the principle of rest, and these two principles of motion and rest permeate life between Heaven and Earth. *Therefore, the Sage talks about rituals and music."*

Finally we arrive at the perception of the profound truth concerning the creation of harmony, and the basis of a great nation. *"Therefore, the superior man tries to create harmony in*

*the human heart by a rediscovery of human nature, and tries
to promote music as a means to the perfection of human culture. When such music prevails and the people's minds are led
toward the right ideals and aspirations, we may see the appearance of a great nation."*

Confucius, I am sure, shares with me the impatience with
the techniques of alimentation and elimination as the means
for solving the present world chaos and planning a world
peace. We are miserably mistaken if we think that Asiatics
can be satisfied with the white man's canned goods. What they
prize are the empty cans because they have a tinkling sound
which pleases the ear and a shining luster which pleases the
soul. For their food, they prefer bananas.

9

MATHEMATICS AND PEACE

WE NEED a larger and subtler vision. I have referred to the
Chinese contempt for the mathematical way of thinking. This
weakness of ancient China was also her greatest strength. All
the important things in life lie somewhat outside the sphere
of the mathematically calculable. It is the incalculables that
count, because it is the incalculables that make us human beings and not the figures of machines. The soul, for instance, is
incalculable; so are God, freedom, decency, self-respect, honesty, pride, and on the other side of the picture, hatred, fear,
revenge, sadism, personal ambition. It is these passions and
their idiosyncratic ways of which we know nothing that upset
human life. You cannot chart their course, but still you have
to make provisions for them. It is these things, about which

the economists and mathematicians have nothing to say, that are important in planning for peace.

Peace is not a mathematical formula and cannot be worked out by mathematical equations. From what has been said about the Confucian theory of government by courtesy and music, it must have become clear that what Chinese thought lost in precision it gained in subtlety. For in all things truly great and utterly small, mathematics is inadequate. It is in measuring astronomical and atomic motions that science is all agog and recognizes that the laws of mathematics fail. And so what is more important than the shape and configuration of the peace after the war is our *method* of arriving at it and our conception of the peace process. Our conception of the peace process is a mathematical one, and the Asiatic contribution to the ideas for creating peace is first of all a challenge to the adequacy of the mathematical approach. Mathematics is cold, but life is warm; that is why mathematics must forever fail to explain life. Reducing the musical note of C to a number of vibrations per second does not explain Lily Pons or Elizabeth Schumann. What explain Lily Pons or Elizabeth Schumann are the overtones which are somewhat beyond mathematical calculations. He who goes for exactness must sacrifice subtlety, and vice versa. Since peace is also a part of life, the mathematical approach must also fail to explain peace, or understand peace, or create it.

In other words, peace cannot be arrived at by a point ration system. The more blurred and indeterminate the natural boundaries, the happier the neighbors are. The less talk about tariff barriers, the greater the flow of trade. The more inexact our delegates' ideas of population figures, the nearer we are to a peace solution. The less concerned the big powers are over the undeveloped areas, the happier are the "natives." The less thought we spend on the diameter of gun barrels, the less imminent is World War III.

That is why I have a hunch that if we leave the planning

of world peace to women, we shall have it, because as the average woman goes, they are pretty bad at figures. A fair precaution to be taken against men delegates to the Peace Conference would be to establish a rule that they must have flunked at school in mathematics to qualify for the appointment or election. Actually even Secretary Hull can think quite sanely and philosophically about the deeper problems of peace if you remove from his company that statistical fiend, Leo Pasvolsky.

For it must never be forgotten that even in the realm of the physical world, science explains the *how*, but never the *why* and the *wherefore*. It deals with the process, but not the ultimate cause, nor the values of the end results. The process lies within the field of mathematics, the values and primary cause lie without. Science explains how the atoms behave, but does not explain why they so behave. It describes how two molecules of sodium and carbon come together, but does not explain why they must come together. It describes acids and alkalis, but cannot say anything about the ultimate acidity of acids. It proves that quinine cures malaria, but does not know why quinine kills the malaria germs. It describes to you the laws of gravitation, but does not pretend to tell you what gravitation is, and why it must be. Before the ultimate Door of Mystery, science always stops short and never enters. It sees acorns sprout and grow into oaks, but cannot tell why they must do so. It observes and proves the survival of the fittest, but cannot account for the arrival of the fittest. It explains how the giraffe survives by his long neck but cannot explain the chemical and physiological process that produced the first long neck. It tells of the survival value of the spotted leopard, but is at a loss about the arrival of the spots. It explains the survival value of the flower's fragrance, but is bashfully silent as to how lilacs and lemons develop their peculiar fragrance. It tells you that silkworms spin silk from mulberry leaves and bees produce honey from nectar and cows produce milk from common grass, and not much else that is really enlightening. For ultimately, bees just produce honey and cows just produce milk and lilacs just create out of the common sod that unmistakable, incomparable perfume. And they all do it simply, finally, and inevitably.

Doubly is this true of the human realm and the realm of the spirit. Christian preoccupation with matter and the materialistic conception of man and of human life and human history arouses in me an uncontrollable heathen rage. I have said that peace on earth is an act of faith, and without faith we shall not be saved. There is almost nothing of value in human life that science can prove, and these human values we have to take on faith. For one thing, the central concept of democracy, the worth and dignity of the individual, can never be proved; science can never prove that the individual is dignified. Cold objectivity fails when a subjective attitude comes in, and human life is 90 per cent attitudes. A woman is a lady when she treats herself as a lady and a whore when she treats herself as a whore. The next minute, a whore can change herself into a lady, by that ultimate hidden process which science must fail to explain—a process which belongs to the secret of life, and which is as impenetrable to science as that by which the lilac manufactures its perfume. Science has nothing to say about human happiness, freedom, and equality, because science does not, and cannot, deal with these human values. Freedom of the will cannot be proved. The possibility of world co-operation cannot be proved. These things have to be proved, not by science, but by faith and by human action. Even the future of the son of a drunkard or a moron or a genius cannot be proved or predicted. The individual always eludes science, and it is only in the mass that the semblance of deterministic laws, like insurance statistics, can be established. But unless the whole view of human society is deterministic, the science of human society cannot even begin. We have to concede either that men and women are helpless pawns of certain mechanical forces, or we must concede that any science of human activities (science of history, or poetry, for instance) is an impossibility.

Therein lies the danger of the mechanical solution of the problem of peace. But the western way of mathematical thinking is established. Hence our present utter confusion—a hundred postwar plans and not one way out. Not one plan gives us the sense of assurance that peace will come. How completely mechanical our way of thinking is may be illustrated by a few personal experiences of mine.

One of the greatest shocks in my college days was when I learned the corpuscular theory of smell. I had thought that smell was just smell, something if not spiritual, at least not corpuscular. I had not troubled to explain it. The idea that smell was transmitted by particles radiating from a body and striking the nerve endings of my nostrils presupposes that these particles constantly radiate in all directions as theoretically visible bodies and fill the air. That may be right and that may be wrong; I have no idea. Maybe moth balls do throw off those bodily particles. But we have to imagine the same of almost all articles and beings, and the air must be chock full of these smell particles. Dogs detect uncanny smells of persons that we are hardly aware of; some must be positively sweet, others repellent. If dogs had a language, they would have a greater variety of words for smell than our highly inadequate words such as "fragrance" and "stench" and the vague one "pungency." Certain smells would blend, like colors, and others would not; it would be even possible to imagine a symphony of smells, as we do of sounds. And all these particles must dance in space. But the theory is on the whole tenable.

When it comes to light, the corpuscular theory is distinctly shaking, for the best professors of light cannot agree on this point. Is light matter, or is it a wave, an impulse, and if the latter, a wave of what? There we are at a dead end. The corpuscular theory raises many theoretic difficulties. If light consists of particles of something, and since two lights in a valley on a dark night hit out in all directions, the two "bodies" must occupy the same space at the same time at any point where the two lights are visible. In the end, that light is a body must seem to the man of the future like some medieval superstition of this mechanical age. At present, we are held down by a mechanical concept because we cannot think of anything without a body. The substance of light is puzzling us. Hence we call it "quantum," which says nothing except that it is a quantity. A quantity of what?

I remember also, while studying under Edouard Sievers, being told that the essential types of rhythm of poetry are twos and threes. Now that is common sense because one syllable does not form a rhythm by itself, and a rhythm of four syllables automatically breaks up into either one and three or into two twos. But that would not be scientific. There is a semi-scientific theory that our sense of rhythm of poetry has a *physical* basis. The two-syllable rhythm is based on the movement of our footsteps—left and right. And how about the three-syllable rhythm? It is based on our respiration—two for exhaling and one for inhaling! This is not science, but what I call the "small talk" of science, the irresponsible rumors. How often professors of the humanities pass from science to scientific small talk the layman is seldom aware—such as the conjecture that the Roman Empire fell because of mosquitoes, which produced malaria! Like society's small talk, these are always pretty and tend to make one prick up one's ears.

Recently, a friend of mine confided to me his theory of time. His theory is that time is not an absolute quantity, but an arbitrary one. For instance, the length of a morning cannot be the same for an insect which lives for only a summer season as it is for a human being who lives seventy or eighty years. I told him that Chuangtse said literally the same thing. But, he said, he had consulted a doctor about this idea, and the doctor had suggested it was probably correct, but that the feeling of time probably had something to do with the rate of the heart beat of the animal! I was stunned. The layman is seldom aware to what extent the small talk, the unprovable assumptions, permeate the so-called human sciences, like psychology, and how largely speculative the whole fabric of psychoanalysis is. (Such as, for instance, the speculative sally that childhood constipation causes stubbornness or miserliness of character, and loose bowels produce the habit of generosity. Shade of Roger Bacon!)

I mention these instances to show how incorrigibly mechanical our present-day way of thinking is. Therefore, it is inevitable that in our thinking of peace we must also confine ourselves to the mechanical barriers, zones, quotas, tonnages, square miles, and population densities, and must perforce neglect the higher and invisible things that alone make peace possible. We have a kind of blind faith in figures. Ely Culbertson typifies this when he transfers his mathematical thinking from contract bridge to the international peace force. Given an international trump card, a "widow," that all parties can call for, and given a certain distribution of cards, he believes that it is impossible for any hand to win against the rest. He does not say anything about the human equation of the bridge players—how one may play recklessly and another may miss a certain chance through sheer preoccupation with a beautiful lady at his side. The game will be like an automatic machine that wins against all.

After the experience of the last war, the Senate of the United States thought there was a sure *mechanical* means of ensuring peace, viz., physical insulation from war areas by the cash-and-carry principle. German submarines sank American ships and American men and goods. That was how America was dragged into war. *Ergo,* the mechanical insulation should lie in not permitting American ships and American goods to sail in war zones! It was simplicity itself. They forgot that there was a human, psychological element: there might be a time when the people would not *want* to apply the cash-and-carry principle, or indeed a time when the people would not stand for its application. And so again, what was built with cards was no stronger than a house of cards. No, neither Arabic figures nor Roman numerals can give us a system of peace. Arabic figures are only good for ration systems or lottery tickets; they may be used as instruments for peace, but they can *never* insure peace.

So I am still for Confucius, and for government by music and by good manners. Confucius passes at once beyond the frontier of the mathematically calculable and goes to the root of social and political order in moral order. He goes even beyond the "political" machinery of law and government and tries to "create harmony in the human heart by a rediscovery of human nature." He points out the strife and chaos resulting from unregulated human desires, that come from the impact of the material world.

> When man is constantly exposed to the things of the material world which affect him and does not control his likes and dislikes, then he is overwhelmed by the material reality and becomes dehumanized or materialistic. When man becomes dehumanized or materialistic, then the principle of Reason in nature is destroyed. From this arise rebellion, disobedience . . .

10

DEFENSE OF COURTESY

AT THIS point, I feel I must offer a defense of government by courtesy and good manners, or government by "rituals." Curiously, the concept of *li* covers both, and extends to the concept of establishing political order by a prevailing sense of moral order, of which the social, religious, and state rituals are to be the symbols.

This prevailing sense of moral order, through establishing the psychological attitude of orderliness, is the philosophic aim of *li,* the central concept of Confucian teachings. For Confucianism was known as the "religion of *li.*" Still, the notion of courtesy, just ordinary social courtesy, remains vivid above the deeper philosophical interpretations. The Chinese call their country "The Country of Courtesy (*li*) and Accommodation (*jang*)." They meant that the Chinese civilization was entitled to the name of civilization in contrast to the surrounding barbarian tribes—and they *were* barbarian tribes—only by virtue of its emphasis on courtesy and accommodation (*"après vous"*), whereas the barbarian tribes to the north, south, east, and west, knew only of fighting one's way through and knew not the culture of letting the other fellow get in first.

We alone knew when to bow once, when to bow twice, and when to bow three times. We called it the mark of civilization. It was to be a country of people whose culture was permeated, whose manners were changed, and whose hearts were influenced, by worship and song (rituals and music). We were to bow and sing on state occasions, bow and sing at village festivals, bow and sing at wedding ceremonies, and bow and sing during archery contests. Through this bowing and singing, our hearts were supposed to be changed, we were to feel refined and civilized, like the lords and ladies at the court of Louis XV. Confucius said of archery contests that the gentleman also entered into contests, but that he "bowed before he went up and drank a cup after he came down. Even at contests, he was a gentleman." Through the ceremonies of worship, secular and religious, we were supposed to imbibe a sense of respect for social order and be taught the attitude of humility in civilized intercourse. Through ancestor worship as a symbolic ritual, the people's attitude of respect for and gratitude toward their elders was to be inculcated and established. Once when Confucius

was assisting the King of Lu at a conference with the King of
Ch'i, he so shamed the neighboring king and his entourage
by Lu's superior manners and classical music that the King of
Ch'i felt like a barbarian, humiliated and disgraced, for Ch'i
offered at the conference music and dance of the Yi barbarians
in what is now eastern Shantung. "When you watch a nation's
dance, you know its character," said Confucius.

Confucius understood mass psychology better than anybody
else. Rituals were symbols, and the masses needed symbols. For
a baron to wear a cap with nine strings of beads or to worship
at Mount Tai, exclusive privileges of the Emperor, would be
not only an insufferable outrage of good manners, but would
be indicative of a rebellious spirit and of social chaos. When a
baron used at his feasts dancers in eight formations, to which
only the Emperor was entitled, instead of in four, which was
proper to a baron, Confucius exclaimed, "If one is to stand for
this, what will one not stand for?"

Since words were also symbols, Confucius developed another
central concept on the correct use of terms. His only book was
a compilation of *Annals (Ch'unch'iu)* with the sole purpose
of restoring a sharp discipline in the correct use of terms and
titles. The idea was that when he wrote down the words
"Baron of Ch'u" (who had called himself "King") in his
Annals, the latter suffered a moral and psychological defeat
and should be shamed out of his disregard for the social and
moral order. It was in this sense that Mencius said of this book
by Confucius that when it was written, "The unruly nobles
and rebellious spirits trembled."

This whole psychological approach to social order is very
curious. It would be a comparatively easy matter for some
Ph.D. candidate to write a thesis on "The Psychology of Confucius" by dressing him up in western terms like the "psychology of habit," "psychology of imitation," "acquired childhood
reflexes," and "mass conditioning by symbols." I am all for
psychology, because it alone holds the key to human behavior,

provided the psychologists could give up its title of a "science" in the sense of a natural science, and confine themselves to sharp and witty observations of human behavior and human motives, as Confucius and William James did.

There is a closer relation between good manners and peace politics than one might think. I know what is war politics and power politics, and I have been somewhat hard put to it to think what is peace politics. Round and round the circle we might go and might not find the answer. Take out the politics of power and of struggle for selfish interests, limited only by the law, and what have we got in its place? Confucianism expresses a huge dissatisfaction with the conception of government by law. For the law always falls one step behind manners and morals; the most charming things men do are always those that rise above legal obligations. "Guide the people with administrative measures and regulate them by the threat of punishments, and the people will try to keep out of jail, but will have no sense of honor. Guide them by morals and regulate them by good manners, and they will have a sense of honor and respect." "In presiding over law-suits I am probably as good as anybody. The point is that there should be no law-suits at all." [17] The conception of legal restraint is postulated on the idea of selfish strife and struggle among the elements of society. Laws cannot stand against bayonets, and when a local or international brigand tears up the law or takes the law into his hands, what have we got to defend the law and defeat the brigand with except those noneconomic and nonmaterial factors—the outraged conscience of mankind? No, we do not escape psychology. Secretary Hull's "orderly processes of negotiation" represent the civilized procedure for international adjustments. But what is the spirit of these "orderly processes"? Polite diplomatic phraseology apart, is it not the spirit of good manners, of courtesy, and accommodation? What do civilized men do, and what should civilized nations do? Will they ac-

---

[17] *Wisdom of Confucius*, p. 198.

commodate? Will they yield to one another? The spirit of
courtesy and accommodation is the very antithesis of the spirit
of strife and contention. It is the true basis of civilized living,
and it is also the only possible basis of a more civilized world
order.

I think the Casablanca Conference failed not merely because
Stalin refused to come, in spite of President Roosevelt's and
Winston Churchill's going to North Africa, instead of meeting
at Washington or Montreal. It failed on the score of bad manners. China's role in this war in 1943, we are told, was discussed, decided upon, and handed out to China. Casablanca
revealed to the whole world that Britain and the United States
intended to run the whole war themselves. That they are not
conscious of their bad manners is more the pity, for they will
be equally unconscious of their bad manners at the peace table.
These do not look like the principles upon which we are going
to build a lasting peace by willing co-operation based on good
manners and mutual respect. One cannot win a war for democracy by dictatorial methods.

The reverse of this case is equally true. China's bowing
in foreign relations has been the cause of misunderstanding
with her Allies. Stemming from courtesy and self-restraint, it
is taken for a sign of weakness. Silence and absence of protests
against the shipping of oil and scrap iron to Japan were taken
to mean profound satisfaction with the state of affairs.

The Stettinius report showed that for the two months of January and February, 1943, Lend-Lease shipments to the United
Kingdom amounted to $470,098,000, to Russia $293,370,00, and
to China $1,067,000. Such a 763:1 ratio means, if the amount
were to be given out in equal daily portions to the three nations by turns, China would have to wait two years, one month
and three days before she got one day's amount. How did
China invite such preposterous contempt? By China bowing
and looking extremely well pleased. An aggressive stenogra-

pher asks for a raise in salary. A good-mannered stenographer never does.

That discrepancy in manners between a well-bred person from a good home, and an aggressive social world where everybody is accustomed to brandishing his fists to get what he wants, is the cause of the whole unmitigated failure of China's foreign policy with her Allies in the last six fighting years. By our kowtowing we were misunderstood. China has been acting like a college freshman just initiated into a fraternity, ready to shake everybody's hand. China must quickly shed her good manners and give somebody a black eye before she can be understood and gain the genuine respect of the fellow members of this strange fraternity. While the smug Allied statesmen still allow themselves to think that the Chinese government and people are extremely grateful to them and are looking up to them as worshipfully as a puppy that has been thrown a piece of dry bone and is perhaps even willing to stand up on its hind legs to entertain the company, some Chinese must tell them the bitter truth. The bitter truth is that behind the courteous front, resentment against the conduct of certain governments is very bitter, that the Chinese are frankly disappointed in their Allies, are getting the impression that their Allies are wholly selfish and insincere and that both Churchill and Roosevelt show no comprehension of the nature of Asiatic problems. They are, moreover, uncertain of what their Allies are fighting for.

The psychology of peace politics is simply this: rough people fight; courteous people don't. Fighting is a social and international disgrace. Courteous men fight sometimes, and when they do fight it is certain that the other party is a barbarian or he is living in a barbarian world with barbarian neighbors, where good manners do not avail. Only good manners, according to Mencius, distinguish men from the beasts.

11

EUROPEANIZATION OF THE WORLD

THE European world is falling apart because its moral values have gone and there is just nothing to hold it together. Nationalism, racial prejudice, militarism (or simple belief in a social order based on force), commercialism, and the development of the machine are breaking it up before our eyes.

Because of the working of these forces in the absence of faith and of a spiritual concept of man, because the economic man has replaced the spiritual man, everything is cracking. Nothing works; nothing guarantees stability. The League of Nations did not work. Disarmament conferences did not work. The Briand-Kellogg Pact, with the solemn signatures of kings and presidents, did not work. International pledges and treaties do not work. The mania for goods and markets and exploitation of material goes on.

So Europe is upsetting the peace of the five continents. Because of Europe and the European current of ideas and Europe's example of imperialism and materialism to other continents, women in Singapore have to die, Burmese villagers' houses have to burn, and peasants in China and in the Caucasus have to watch bombs falling on their fields.

But being itself a slaughterhouse, Europe is now planning to transform Asia and Africa into a gigantic slaughterhouse. It still thinks that the world owes Europe a debt, and that the world has to come up to European standards of living. Europe, I know, still intends to appropriate the world. There are the British Empire, the French Empire, and the Dutch Empire. Even Portugal has got a concession, Macao, in China! Thank God the Spanish Empire has crumbled and collapsed, otherwise we would have just as complicated problems in South America.

Today Asia and Africa must still be the cows that produce the milk for Europeans. Why? Because Europe wants to raise their standards of living and educate them toward self-government! Who in the first place robbed them of their liberty and their self-government? Who says that the standards of living in India have improved, and not deteriorated, after two centuries of English rule? Sir Norman Angell dares not contradict the fact that the abject poverty of the Indian peasants is worse than even that of seventy years ago, owing to English exploitation and the killing of native industries. While I am writing this, the boast of some English bureaucrats in India, "the situation is well in hand," keeps ringing in my ears. I see the Empire breaking, but unwillingly. But unless the Empire breaks itself, the issue of Empire will break the Allies and the Peace Conference and render futile all that men are dying for now.

But at present, the Europeanization of the world is not just an idea, an abstraction. The democratic leaders of the world are transferring to Asia their sin-smelling and strife-breeding power politics, with the sure result that Asia, by means of a prepared and planned balance of power, will be kept in continual bloodshed and strife and mutual slaughter for the next three centuries, after Europe's noble example. Europe is the focus of infection on this earth, and its toxin spreads through all the five continents. When will the plague burn itself out? Why cannot Europe leave Asia alone? How can we quarantine Europe? How, in other words, quarantine European power politics? I shall be able to show that without European interference, the problems of the future of Asia after the war are quite simple. With the British, French, and Dutch Empires, the problems of Asia will become as complicated as those of Europe itself after the war.

And here, before I go on, I must make an exception for the lambs of Europe and separate them from the wolves. I mean the Norwegians, the Swedes, the Danes, the Swiss, who wish nobody any harm and who are pioneers in social legislation and standards of enlightenment. The Dutch, the Belgians, and the English are splendid people when they stay at home. The compelling tradition of social decency is so great that all you need to do to make an Englishman a gentleman again is to ship him back west of the Suez Canal. Really the white man is quite charming when he has got rid of his "burden." He can even discuss Walter Pater with you.

But what are you going to Europeanize the world with? The better knowledge of vitamins and nutrition, child care, maternity care, and better foundations for women's dress are conceded. Don't worry about those. The women of Turkey, Iraq, Iran, China, and the Congo will bless you for these things and gladly pay homage to Europe without question. But what are you going to Europeanize the world with? The European standards of living, of course. Curious that one does not say the standards of morals. Nobody dares to suggest that the standards of morals and of thinking of the East or of the West be raised. No, it is not the gospel of high thinking and simple living that the economic man is the apostle of. Rather the gospel of high living and fairly simple thinking, such simple thinking as that material prosperity brings happiness, or that the industrial man is happier than the craftsman. When one speaks of raising the standards of living, one means clearly and simply that laundry will be more pleasant, and dish-washing and vacuum-cleaning will be easier on the housewife, plus perhaps a quart of milk a day for the Hottentot. One means less hand labor. One means having a car and seeing a movie once a week. One means exactly these things.

The message of raising the standards of living of the world means simply that you want to move the people of the East End and all the world to Park Avenue. But suppose the people of the East End do not like Park Avenue and prefer to remain where they are. Have they lost something important, and what have they lost? Suppose the Hottentot does not care for your quart of milk, and prefers bananas? Suppose the Oriental man does not share your ideas of hand labor and the Oriental woman does not mind washing her clothes on a river bank while chatting with her neighbors, and thinks it pleasanter than washing by a machine in a hot, steaming cellar? Suppose the Oriental man does not think it is such a bad thing to wade knee-deep in rice paddies and plough his land, son in front and father behind? Suppose he believes it is good for the body and the soul to use his hands in work and his bare legs in walking? Suppose a man who lives in a mud hut of bare walls and pushes a hand cart and therefore has a lower "standard of living" is not necessarily living like a pig, as Occidental tourists constantly assume? Suppose he has the culture of a self-respecting man? Suppose he believes in paddling his boat instead of riding a steamboat chugging its way through the water, all the while feeling guilty inside of being corrupted by European standards of ease and idleness? Suppose he prefers his wife to make her own cloth shoes instead of wearing expensive leather shoes that only idle city women can afford? Suppose he believes in mothers nursing their own babies, even in public? Suppose he does not think nursing a baby in public is an indecent, immoral, and lewd spectacle, according to the code of Will Hays, because the true function of the woman's breasts has not been corrupted in him? Suppose he perceives the subtle physiological truth that the human body is capable of infinite adjustments, that habitual comforts cease to have meaning, and that the hard life is probably healthier than the easy life? Suppose the Seventh Heaven is in a Parisian attic to be ascended by dingy stone stairs? Suppose it is a human truth that a poor newspaper boy is physically, mentally, and morally having a happier childhood than a rich man's son on Park Avenue learning to skate with James the Butler and Charles the Doorman holding him up by each arm? In other words, suppose material standards of living are not worth raising at all—at the price of increasing class hatred, increasing collectivism, loss of individual freedom, and periodic conscripting of boys of eighteen for war?

At bottom, I believe, the modern European is as superstitious as any Asiatic. The over-all superstition that is an intellectual fad in the present era is belief in determinism, and that man is primarily an animal, governed, shaped and controlled helplessly by material environment. Besides the supreme god of determinism, there are also some fetishes that the modern man worships. I call a superstition any belief in something untrue, and I call a fetish whatever a man worships beyond its proper value. The three European fetishes are, the Potato Fetish, the Population Fetish, and the Power Fetish. For verily these are the gods of the modern era. Man is superstitious anyway; take away his *ikon* and he must worship something else. Emotionally, he has to be oriented somewhere. He who does not worship something is lost. Even an atheist must worship his mistress's ankles.

It is these three fetishes that are molding men's thoughts about the peace, based on the following axioms: (1) Men live by potatoes. Metaphysically, man is a biped searching for potatoes, and human civilization is that aggregate historical force arising out of the biped's search in the direction of potato supplies. (2) The lack of potatoes is the cause of war, and the possession of potatoes is the guarantee of peace. The more potatoes you have, the more civilized you are, when you can spell out happily the word "Prosperity." (3) The technique of peace lies in finding and providing the exact ratio between populations and potatoes. (4) Those who don't have power must grow potatoes, and those who have power may eat, transport, and otherwise dispose of the potatoes that the others grow. (5) As is evident from a natural law, those who have power must see that those who don't have power grow enough potatoes for the others, or mankind will starve. There must be free access to potatoes, there must be economic planning, and somebody must rule the world. (6) War will not arise between those who have power and those who don't. The potato or agricultural group is by nature stationary and pacifist; the power or industrial group is by nature aggressive, competitive, and predatory. Consequently, the members of the potato-growing group are very cute and lovable and you may now and then pinch their cheeks, but they need not be taken into consideration. (7) War will arise, however, from the allocation among the power groups of the potato supplies raised by the nonpower groups. (8) Peace, it follows logically, is merely a question of the equitable distribution of potato supplies among the power groups. (9) Inasmuch as the power groups are divided among themselves and by nature suspicious of each other and business is by its nature competitive, aggressive, and predatory, the obvious solution is to keep the power so evenly and delicately balanced that none of them will dare fire the first shot, although it may be conceded that someone may. (10) Since power is dynamic and never static, this balance of power can never be permanently maintained; constant adjustments and new alignments are necessary. (11) The technique of constantly watching out for a rising or new power and making new alignments is called "politics"; the method of switching about alignments and double-crossing former allies, up to the moment the first shot is fired, is called "diplomacy"; the final upset of that delicate and unstable balance is called "war." (12) This is not very satisfactory, but obviously there is nothing better. (13) A really satisfactory and a most desirable solution would be for one power or combination of powers to acquire sufficient power to dominate the rest in some sort of World Democracy. If the other power groups or potato groups don't like it, what are they going to do about it? We've got better guns and more guns. (14) Damn it, we are honest. We are "realists" who tell no "fairy tales" to deceive the people, while the others who talk about justice and kindness as if they meant it are "visionaries."

This is the high plane of international thinking about peace problems in the year of our Lord 1943. It is the sum total of our political wisdom. These tenets of thinking, when applied to Europe, have produced European chaos and bloodshed for centuries. The belief is, however, that when they are applied to the world, they will produce World Peace. This is the meaning of the Europeanization of the world.

12

DEFENSE OF THE MOB

AM I not painting too somber a picture of the modern world and of the content of modern civilization? Have I not overlooked something? And have I not exaggerated a bit, or at best concentrated on the dark side of things? The reply is of course that I have; but I am talking of politics, and politics is the dark side of anything; it is the seat bottom of any people's culture. Every culture has a cheery face, too, besides a pants' seat. Perhaps I have been kicking merely at the pants' seat— alas, a foolish occupation!

For Europe is a bull, and I am merely its "gadfly" in the Socratic sense. Liberals, in my opinion, should be merely gadflies to sting the buttocks of the wise and mighty bull which is the state, and thus perform an extremely useful function. For the old bull, after having grazed idly in the mountain pastures, and getting a little bulky and fat, constantly tends to doze off in the midst of danger. Its muscles are a little flabby and its hide gets thicker and thicker. The gadfly buzzes and buzzes and would give it no rest, and gets hated for its pains or perhaps receives a lash from the sweep of the censorial oxtail. What matter, if it has delivered its sting and kept the old, wise bull awake?

No; rather I am conscious of the hopes and dreams and sweet longings and the impulses for good in any people. That is why I am writing this book. When you have an ideal beautiful as a flower, and when you see somebody crush that flower, you feel it like a wound in your heart. Millions of men and women are feeling that pain also, and even some resentment against the person who crushes that flower.

For every war is a discovery of the people. Dunkirk is a discovery of the English people; Stalingrad is a discovery of the Russian people; Bataan, a discovery of the American people; and Chungking, a discovery of the Chinese people. Certain truths about the people tend to be continually forgotten and are rediscovered only under the stress of war. The people have certain qualities that have nothing to do with the workings in the dark chambers of high politics, or with the degenerate, sophisticated literary circles. There is more truth, kindness, heroism, romance, humor, pathos, more depth and richness of life in a country doctor's office than in the Foreign Office of any nation; and it is of this truth, heroism, romance, and humor and pathos that the stuff of life is made, and by which the stream of human life is carried on.

When I see on the screen pictures of Russian peasant women helping to defend their country, English air wardens and women police and nurses, American women making shoes for the army—when I see the efforts of the common people, volunteers, nurses, WAVES, WAACS, workmen, truck-drivers, welders, machinists, working at the wheel, at the shipyard, the canteen, the factory, the ferry command, I know it is the expression of the will of the people, coming out of the goodness of their hearts, and I respect that will and am impressed by it. They not only say that they are fighting for a better and kindlier world and a better and kindlier society, they *believe* it. And they not only believe it, they want it. They not only want it, but passionately desire it, and are willing to fight and die for it.

So it is in the United States, and so it is in England and China and Russia. The people want peace, a just peace, and good will toward men. There is plenty of good will lying about. Any people, particularly the illiterate and "ignorant" peasantry, have certain old, honorable, sterling qualities, a certain sense of right and wrong, of obligation and duty, that they live by. The present war is a discovery of the *laopaishing* of China, of the peasants of Russia, the commoners of England, and the people, the real people, of America. Not one of them cares a rap about imperialism; not one of them does not wish for surcease from sorrow and wars and contentions in this world. The people want peace. Why can't they have it?

And here we run into an intellectual dilemma of modern democracy. If the people are sound at heart, if they desire peace, and if at the same time they are living in a democracy, why cannot the will of the people be effective? Has not somebody been cheating them, and if so, who? And by what method and on what terms are the people of even a modern democracy being cheated? Briefly, the answer lies in the fact that there is a growing tendency to hand over the government of the country to bureaucrats and "experts," and the terms on which the people are told to surrender their judgment to them are that these experts have "all the facts," which the people, the poor laymen, are not supposed to have. This is perhaps natural in view of the growing complexity of modern problems, but it also means that we are losing faith in the common man—an unhealthy, undemocratic tendency.

So I must come to the defense of the mob. The people of the modern world are always a little scared of specialist learning, particularly of some special "facts," such as the bureaucratic experts say they have and the people do not have. This is a curious phenomenon of modern democracy: to shout merely "I have all the facts" is enough to scare the people into surrender of all judgment. Although this in itself has nothing to do with objective science, the unquestioning respect for "facts" is based on it. By claiming possession of "facts" alone, the prestige of science is at once transferred to the bureaucracy of the political élite, and a halo of sanctity descends upon it. Unless the nature of "facts" in human history is critically examined and the confusion of the facts of physical science with the facts of human society is dispelled, the public in a modern democracy will always be at the mercy of the specialists and experts, economic and political, and that is the ruin of the universe. A layman is a man who suggests that a thing can be done, and an expert is one who knows exactly how a thing can't be done. Consequently, peace experts are people who try to convince you that there can be no peace. Consequently, if you leave peace in the hands of the experts, we shall have to go on fighting forever.

Evidently, there is a difference between a physical fact and a social or political fact. When we say carbon and oxygen combine to form carbon monoxide or carbon dioxide, that is a fact, ascertained and final. Take, however, a social fact, as in a court trial, for example, in which the best means of establishing evidence known to men are applied. The question is whether a man is guilty or not. The facts are reviewed, arguments rehearsed, and a summary is given by the judge. A jury of twelve sits and deliberates and a verdict is delivered, and the accused is pronounced "guilty" or "not guilty." But the fact of his guilt is evidently different from the fact of carbon dioxide. Probably seven jurors have believed he is guilty and five have believed him innocent, whereas it is impossible by a vote among scientists to pronounce a substance carbon monoxide or carbon dioxide. In strictly scientific terms, the "fact" of his guilt would be no more than a fair surmise or hypothesis, on fairly ample or insufficient grounds. The difference is that the natural scientist can reserve judgment on a piece of substance or a phenomenon, whereas in human affairs a decision, a choice, has to be made at a given date.

Again in human affairs, an individual fact may be ascertained or established scientifically, but a social fact is always an inference, like the jury's verdict of "guilty" or "not guilty." Of course, if a man commits a murder in Times Square and he is caught in the act, that is a fact, even a scientific fact. Unfortunately, the "facts" which our diplomats and experts tell us they "have" are not of this order, but are primarily judgments and evaluations of great social forces of a highly complex nature. Such facts are always many-sided and multi-colored and open to the most diverse interpretations.

But we are confused; we dare not trust ourselves. Who dares challenge the experts' opinions on India, or on the handling of North African affairs? Is Gandhi an appeaser, or is he a saint? Were the French people of North Africa for Darlan or De Gaulle? How can we people ever know? Is it not the part of wisdom to reserve judgment? No, the people's instinct is always right, for the people always rely on first principles. For nothing is plain in this world except first principles. Furthermore, there are no facts of history that any man ever comprehends in their entirety. Listen to Robert Murphy and to a correspondent from North Africa, and you know it can never be proved whether the "people" who were for Darlan are the royalist rich refugees or the real people of France. Statesmen can publish their memoirs and journalists can record conversations with all classes of people, and you may be sure that social "facts"—e.g., the prevalent sentiment in North Africa and how it may be brought to light by a strong leadership and what are the psychological repercussions in France of alternate policies— are a blending of judgments, prejudices, and piecemeal information. Such facts of history are generally as clear to the mind of the average diplomat as the surface of the moon is to the naked eye. One swears that there is a rabbit, another that there is a monkey, and still another that there is a frog in the moon. It is of such facts the diplomats speak when they tell you they have "all" of them. The fact is, the poor mortals sitting in their mouse holes or debating about the rabbit, the monkey, and the frog are as confused about them as we are. In fact, they are more confused by the steady gazing and squinting at the moon. So when they try to shut you up by saying, "I tell you it is a rabbit—I know," you should give them the satisfaction of their pride and self-respect, but keep for yourself a healthy suspicion that their eyes have been somewhat exercised over it. You should reserve for yourself the first principles, which are that there are lights and shadows on the moon, and that Darlan and Peyrouton and all Vichyites are the shadows while the people of France are the light. If you say right is right and wrong is wrong, you may be sure that you are right. You know you are the mob, and the mob is always right, and be happy about it.

It has sometimes seemed to me that we don't need the Four Freedoms, but only one Freedom—Freedom from Humbug. The supreme modern humbug is that the mere possession of facts is a good excuse and justification for dispensing with principles. Remember only one thing: the experts have all the facts, while the people have all the judgment. This faith must not be shaken, for when it is shaken, democracy falls into the hands of the experts, and when democracy falls into the hands of the experts, democracy just falls. For God speaks through the people, and through the people alone.

I have a feeling that God always works through the mob. The mob, after all, has a certain Divine Right. My inspiration does not necessarily come from the Chinese *Book of History,* which says, "God listens through the ears of the people and speaks through the mouth of the people." It comes from an intuitive insight and from my observation of history. When the mob is resentful, it is God who is resentful. When the mob is enraged, be sure God is enraged. When the mob is violent and uses the guillotine, it is God who thinks it is time to be violent and invent the guillotine. When the mob hesitates, it is God who hesitates. And when the mob goes back to its homes to pursue the daily business of life, it is God who is happy.

Therefore when the public sentiment condemns a public policy, it is God who condemns it. When public sentiment revolts against Hitler's doctrine of power, it is God who revolts. Only be sure that while God works with the mob, the devil works through the experts and provides them with "all the facts." Who can be sure that the "facts" which American officials have about North Africa are not ghosts in the cabinet that the devil has put there by his magic? We all enjoy the polite fables that in a department store the customer is always right, in a monarchy the king is always right, and in a democracy the Foreign Office is always right. For the people believe in honest dealings and the principles of right; diplomats prowl in secret like owls at night, and are happiest in darkness. The struggle between the people and the diplomats in any nation is, and must always be, the struggle between God and the devil, between the powers of darkness and of light. Spell "Cliveden" backward, and you will find a devil in it.

It was not the people of England and France who crucified the Spanish Loyalists and put them in concentration camps; it was their governments that did it. It was not the people of England and France who set up the Non-Intervention Committee and connived at Hitler's and Mussolini's open intervention; it was their governments. The only real "facts" in the situation are that the Cliveden set of England and the Lavals of France feared and hated Communism more than they feared and hated Hitler. It was not the people of America who embargoed the supply of oil to Republican Spain; it was the Government of the United States of America that did it. It was not the people of England who gave Japan a free hand in Manchuria and Mussolini a free hand in Ethiopia; it was the public officials of the League of Nations who did it. It is not the people who wish to delay definition of freedom for the people of the earth after the war and say "Win the war first"; it is the governments that are doing so.

I am not convinced that all the idiots lived in the past and the great extraordinary minds live only in the present. History has repeatedly proved governments to have been stupid and wrong and the moral instinct of the people to have been right. If the governments could be wrong in the past decade, they can be wrong now. Be a gadfly, therefore, and sting the governments.

But it is almost a law of human nature that we have all the rights and privileges to sting a dead statesman, like Neville Chamberlain, but not the living great of this earth. When the harm is done and belongs to the past decades, when the sufferings and wrongs of the people are mere memories, pointing out mistakes is a luxury of the reminiscent historian whose voice is calm and tinged with an exquisite regret. When the mistakes are being committed before our eyes, to point out the mistakes and errors of the living great is to arouse all the ire of the red-hot patriots.

In a democracy, however, there is always hope. For leadership in a democracy always consists in marking time and being pushed by the people from behind. There the great leader stands, with a glad eye cast on the right and a twinkling eye on the left, while he marks time with his steps. If he is pushed hard enough from the right, he totters to the left, and if he is pushed hard enough from the left, he totters to the right. Only thus is he able to lead the people. And if he is successfully pushed in the direction we want him to go, we acclaim him a "great man." That is why I love democracy, for I enjoy pushing around our leaders, and why I detest tyrants, for I resent being pushed around. There is hope yet in democracy, for if we the people push hard enough this time, out of this war will yet emerge one of the greatest leaders of democracy. Someday a White Paper will be published, and like the old forgetful actor who resented the prompter's voice during the performance, it will say to the people after the show, "You presumptuous, meddlesome fool! I knew perfectly well all the time what I was doing." And the people will again say to him like the prompter, "Of course, you did. You were, as always, perfectly magnificent, Horatio!"

That is why I am writing this book, to do a little prompting and gadfly-stinging and pushing our great leaders toward their inevitable Destiny and their Niche in History. And when the victory is over, they will smile upon us from the stage with a triumphal smile, and we shall acclaim them from below, and they will wave their hats in return. But in applauding them, we shall be applauding ourselves and we shall be feeling happy that they have been gladly pushed in our direction. For if democracy has any real meaning, it is that it is we the people who shall have won the war—let the applause go to our illustrious, extraordinary great minds.

Besides this unhealthy tendency to hand over the government of a nation to an impersonal, anonymous political élite, there is another purely political device by which the will of the common people can be easily defeated or circumvented even in a modern democracy. As I watch the interplay of public opinion and government policy in the foremost modern republic, the United States of America, it is interesting to note that it is entirely possible for a handful of men, some known and some unknown, to get around the will of the people, to carry on with no foreign policy, or even with a foreign policy directly contradictory to the public sentiment of the people. Even with the facilities of a free press, it always takes considerable time for the public to catch up to what the government is doing or not doing. This results in a time lag between public opinion and policy, of six months or a year; but by proper application of a device, this time lag can be made to cover several years.

As this time lag between the will of the people and a nation's effective policy is not only natural but has become quite a feature of modern republics, let us study some instances and see how it works. People may be puzzled about how the popular will of American democracy for aid to China could have been so successfully and adroitly parried over six years. The working of this device will enlighten us. It always took about a year for the public to catch on to what President Roosevelt was doing and not doing, and for President Roosevelt to catch on to public intolerance of the situation. And here I should make it clear that, as a foreigner, I have, as a matter of general courtesy, no right to criticize any government not my own in regard to its domestic issues and policies. I do think, however, that among allies at war, every citizen has the right and the duty to criticize the conduct of allied governments in matters that concern the common war, and particularly in matters that concern and affect the war in his own country. I further think that such mutual criticism is not only permissible, but decidedly healthy, and preferable to a false sense of courtesy. Only in the same spirit in which I would welcome criticism from Englishmen and Americans of such conduct of the Chinese Government as affects the common war, would I presume to say things about foreign governments in matters that directly affect my own country. In fact, I should be highly appreciative if an Allied citizen would point out wherein the conduct of the Chinese Government is slowing down the war with Japan and, by such frank criticism, lessen the cost of Chinese lives before the war with Japan is won. I believe true international understanding can be based only on such a frank and healthy exchange of opinion.

When the public was sufficiently aroused over the shipping of iron and oil to Japan to bomb Chinese women and children, after this had been going on for four years, it was time to take some action. A "license" system was invented and the public was lulled into silence, on the assumption that the license system was meant to operate in restricting oil and iron to an aggressor. It took fully a year for the knowledge to penetrate into the public consciousness that every license the Japanese applied for was granted by the State Department and that the total of oil shipped to Japan had increased three times instead of diminishing. The public reserved judgment because the State Department had "all the facts" and reserved them for their own knowledge. In time, this was exposed and stopped.

Then the Burma Road was permitted to be closed. Public sentiment wanted the supplies to China continued, and President Roosevelt therefore announced that America "would find the means" to replace the Burma Road. The public was lulled into silence again on the assumption that adequate air transport was being provided, or at least planned, and the line of propaganda was put out that air transport, sufficiently developed, could carry the same volume as the Burma Road. As late as January, 1943, President Roosevelt tried to lull the public by stating a literal truth, that the air transport was carrying into China as much as ever traversed the Burma Road. This literal truth had the ring of a Pond's Cold Cream advertisement: "She is engaged. She uses Pond's." No one dared to specify the tonnage carried in; but I knew, and many Chinese at Kunming and correspondents in India knew. The people did not catch on to what President Roosevelt meant till a month or two later. Now the public knows it. Now the scandalous situation is conceded; something has got to be done. If an airplane can carry one pair of slippers into China, ten airplanes can carry ten pairs. But no, the propaganda line is completely reversed. President Roosevelt and others completely contradicted what he had said a year ago. It is being drummed into our ears that the Himalayas are too high, every plane has to carry its return fuel, there are always rains and storms, and only a land route can be satisfactory. Some air transports will of course be added to pacify the public, and to be able to say we are flying in more "than the last month for which complete reports are available." But we must wait for the reopening of the Burma Road.

The public is lulled into silence once more by the assumption that plans for recapture of the Burma Road have already been set. Besides, General Wavell started the march toward Akyab unilaterally to silence the demand for action in Burma. Now we are in for another lag, and it will not be till a year from now that the public will realize there is no plan and no date for concerted action in Burma fully a year after China was cut off. The public does not know that concerted action is necessary and Burma cannot be recaptured without the co-operation of the British Navy in the Bay of Bengal. President Roosevelt said we would help China as quickly as the Lord will let us. The public does not know and President Roosevelt did not explain that the "Lord's" name is Churchill and his first name is Winston. It will take a year before the idea seeps in.

Anyway, while the American people are both friendly to China and sincere in their wish to help China in this war, the policy and acts of their Government are such as to suggest complete indifference in the whole six years of the China War, both before and after Pearl Harbor. Casablanca also condemned China to at least four more years of intense suffering and strangulation with the same cold indifference. The fact that China was the first to fight the Fascists, that she has fought single-handed for six years already, that she is condemned to a total of ten years of war with Japan, that in the coming four years, the Chinese people will be going through an unbearable and steadily mounting inflation, general malnutrition, and a double economic blockade by her enemy on the east and her friends on the southwest—these facts have not bothered the heads of western democracies. But, as I told my people in 1940, we must distinguish between the American government and the American people, even as we must distinguish between the German government and the German nation.

It is fair to point out here that if the same dilatory tactics applied to the problem of getting supplies to China had been applied to the problem of getting scrap iron and oil to Japan, it could have been equally successful, and Japan might now have a dozen million gallons less of gasoline and seven million tons less of first-grade scrap iron to fight America with. On the other hand, if getting supplies to China had been handled with half the alacrity and cheerfulness with which permits for shipments of scrap iron and oil to Japan were granted by the American State Department, and if there had been such a smooth-running machine for giving aid to China since 1939 as for giving aid to Japan, China would now already have the striking offensive power to drive the Japanese into the sea without the sacrifice of American soldiers' lives.

It should be clearly understood that I am not one given to grumbling; when other powers help China, I do not hesitate to express my appreciation. In the first years of the China War, Russia gave China supplies cheerfully, speedily, and in generous volume, and Germany herself gave supplies to China cheerfully, speedily, and in generous volume. What had to be done was done efficiently. Particularly orders from Germany arrived in China in characteristic German fashion, with every detail worked out and provided for, with full repair parts and ammunition and oil for a full year's supply and upkeep for each unit, and with blueprints, instructions, and assembly technicians. When the hundred American P—40's were given to China, they were deprived of their radio sets, and a Chinese company had to cast about and order their own. And if you knew the story of how China was to obtain an assembly man for an airplane that arrived somewhere in India, you would weep. After September, 1939, China could not get a hairpin from Washington without British consent; everywhere she ran up against British priority.

In time of war, there is also an artificial time lag, for, according to our rulers, anything except the arrival of the morning sun in the east is a "military secret." There is always a sensational hush-hush about something being cooked up in the private chambers inside long dark corridors where grown-up

men move about respectfully and therefore silently and dare
only whisper. Like a pale, tender, ailing infant, the foreign
policy of a nation may be spoken of only in a whisper, and the
slightest draft of public knowledge will blow out its tender
young life. Poor infant, there it lies swaddled in stifling clothes
in an overheated suffocating room, and its father is a man-
diplomat slithering about in white gloves and patent-leather
pumps with perspiration on his head. Oh, diplomat-father,
hand back the baby to its mother, the people. Pull the blinds
up, so that she may see better. Perhaps the thing in the swad-
dling clothes being hatched out in the darkness of diplomatic
and "military" secrecy is only a squeaky little mouse or a young
chipmunk.

Wilson was right: there should be no secret diplomacy. And
Wilson was wrong: there can be no open diplomacy. Let's take
a look at his "facts" and see how a foreign policy is hatched
out in the dark without the help of the "mob."

For thus goes the day of the diplomat. Properly ensconced
on the top floor and comfortably inaccessible to the public, he
sits in his hard, upright, high-backed chair that used to belong
to the nephew of Louis Napoleon. On the side of the room
there is a long, plain table that comes from a very old Aragon
family of Spain. The room is richly and, what is more important, heavily curtained. There is an atmosphere of complete
silence, broken by *tick-ticks* from the secretary's room. It is
insulated from the world, and yet it is not; there is on the
other hand, an air of intense excitement and power. In a spe-
cially built enclosure is a wireless telephone that will put him
in instant touch with some distant continent.

And this happened: He arrived at half-past nine. The safe
and tight-lipped stenographer who had looked beautiful twenty
years ago tiptoed in and whispered, "C. from Brazil has an
appointment with you and has already arrived." "Show him in
to Room C," said the diplomat. "The First Secretary is whispering there with the Bishop who has a message from the Vati-

can." "Room B, then," said the diplomat. "Room B is also occupied. The military attaché is whispering there with Captain John of Somnoveria." "Take him to Room A." The elderly secretary's brows lifted and she replied, with the pencil on her lips, "Are you sure, sir, you want to talk to him there? It faces the east and the morning sun shines directly into the room. You know only the young stenographers see their callers there, and it may be inconvenient." The first great problem of the day had already come up, but the day was young and he would not be upset. He gave the final instruction, "Show him right in here, then!"

The secretary tiptoed out and C. of Brazil tiptoed in. You could have heard a pin drop, and the diplomat heard his own stuffed shirt perceptibly move against his underwear as he breathed. The conversation began with "It is a bright day, isn't it?" and ended with a low whisper, "Ah, very interesting, how very interesting!"

The second and the third interviews ended with more "Ah, very interesting's" in still lower whispers. The world in fact was getting very interesting, made more interesting by a wireless telephone call from Stockholm. Now it became positively amazing. He called Ankara. It was now astonishing. Never in one day had he obtained so much interesting information or learned so many secrets. He remembered having read somewhere a Chinese proverb, "A gentleman never steps outside his threshold and knows all that is happening under heaven," and appreciated its obvious truth. He was sure he knew all the facts —in fact, he knew too many. He had known all the facts all along. What to do with them was the problem.

About five o'clock in the afternoon, he received another secret report from Berne, which his secretaries had just decoded. Again he was muttering, "How very interesting!" when he was unpleasantly reminded that there was a press conference set at 5:15. What was he to say? That worried him—very much. He must not let the cat out of the bag. "Can't you tell them I've a sore throat?" he asked the secretary, really seeking her advice. "That would be a poor excuse. Oh, you big boy, you know what to say," said Dorothy adoringly. "I have so many facts that I am utterly confused—bewildered is the word," he muttered, still searching for light. Surveying his well-parted hair, Dorothy said, "The inside of your brain appears less orderly than the outside. . . . Courage, sir, you have handled the rabble before. Broad generalities are always safe. And whenever it becomes awkward, there's the *war* . . ." Dorothy's voice lifted toward the end.

Armed with the air of military secrecy, he went forth to battle. He never failed in combat. At the critical moment, he barked, "I know all the facts." The argument was unanswerable. The diplomat had all the facts, the press did not have them; the public felt beaten in an unfair game. He could not tell the facts, moreover, except in a White Paper to be issued four years hence which the press correspondents would be at liberty to challenge then if they liked. . . . So another day began and ended, as many days had begun and ended, with a whisper in his heart, "Ah, how very interesting!"

It had been interesting like this years before. The diplomat had all the facts in 1931 during the Manchurian Incident. He had all the facts during the Spanish War. He had all the facts during the war in Ethiopia. He had all the facts when Hitler marched into the Ruhr district. He had the facts at Munich. He had the facts when the *Panay* was bombed, when Hainan was occupied, when Japan moved into Indo-China, when the Pearl Harbor attack was being planned. Alas, nobody questions the facts. But what did he do with them?

But if the people are kept behind the facts, events move always ahead of them. Without the first principles which the common people have, every new fact and every new event bring a new confusion. Let's deal only with the facts and not with the first principles—win the war first. But North Africa was invaded and created interesting problems without first principles to meet them. The Russians drove the Nazis from Stalingrad. There was a new problem. The Russians drove past Kursk and Kharkov. The shadow of Russia's rising power loomed larger. The Russians reached Rostov and passed Rzhev. The problem pressed closer home. Will the Russians quit at the frontiers? What a problem! Or will they advance to Berlin? A worse problem still! The exiled government of Poland has split with Sikorski. What an interesting fact! Czechoslovakia's mind is divided. Another interesting fact! Stalin's order of the day—a fact, yet not so interesting because the public already knows it. Von Papen in Ankara. What an interesting fact! Stalin is urging the Polish guerrillas to start fighting, while the exiled governments in London are urging them not to fight and waste their strength for the time being. Another interesting fact! *Hush, hush. . . .* So the facts keep chasing after the week's rising and fast developing events, the diplomats keep chasing after the facts, and the people keep chasing after the diplomats, and the public is always six months or twelve months behind. And our leaders still say, Win the war first! Deal only with the facts!

Facts are always complicated; first principles are always simple. Without first principles, the facts overwhelm us and must continue to overwhelm us, straight to the day when the Allies shall sit down at the Peace Conference table. Facts are unknowable, the only things we can be certain about are principles and ideas. That is why men acting without principles must always be confused. The principle of gravitation harmonizes all heavenly motions; the principle of love harmonizes all earthly growth; and only the principles of sincerity and justice can solve the problems of world politics. The war calls for a moral leadership, a leadership that rests on first principles. It calls for a man with the mind of Lincoln, with its simplicity and its strength. But we are so busy throwing up and laying bricks to build the second and third floors that we are perfectly contented to think about the foundation afterward. And we are surprised that the bricks we laid on with so much pathetic effort yesterday always threaten to go out of plumb today.

And so the problem of Russia frightens us. The problem of Poland frightens us. The problems of Rumania and Czechoslovakia and the Baltic States frighten us. The problems of India and Hong Kong frighten us. Above all the application of the Atlantic Charter frightens us. We had meant to win the war first, and talk about the peace afterward. But time does not wait, and peace refuses to be kept waiting. Time waits for no man, not even for democratic leaders. Meanwhile we can only pray that God will temper the wind of events to our shorn diplomat-lamb.

13

THE FUTURE OF ASIA

UNFORTUNATELY, God will not temper the wind. Poor lamb, you'd better grow your wool fast.

I see nothing but starvation and chaos and bloodshed in Asia. I know our policy in Asia will grow into a disaster, with mounting confusion before the war is over. In the war councils of today, there is a blind spot, and that spot is Asia. The same absent-mindedness that characterized the situation suggested in General Arnold's speech at Madison Square Garden on March 6, 1943, will continue to characterize the Allied policy in Asia. As we refuse to think about postwar problems now, so we refuse to think about Asia until the war is won. General Arnold said, "Six weeks ago at Casablanca . . . I headed for the Far East. Before departure, President Roosevelt expressed himself briefly, 'China's ports are closed, the Japanese hold the Burma Road. How can we increase the air tonnage carried in?

How can we build a larger combat force?'" I thought that President Roosevelt had known that China's ports were closed a year before Casablanca. Thoughtfulness of this type really resembles forgetfulness. I thought this must have occurred to anyone who ever spent a minute's thought on the strategy of fighting Japan from China. How could the most obvious fact on the map of the Orient be forgotten, and why up to now is there no plan, and *no wish for a plan,* for China's partnership even in the war against Japan?

Meanwhile, General Arnold in the same speech made it amply clear that increase of air transport will be difficult, for supplying the China-India front means taking planes out of the other fronts. There will be more planes sent to China as a gesture to pacify the American public, so that the public will be lulled into silence, but the basic policy will be unchanged. Everything, we shall be told, will depend upon the reopening of the Burma Road, but we are awfully sorry we cannot spare the British Navy to land troops at Rangoon. The difficult we do immediately, the impossible a little later on. China belongs to the impossible. And we adore the Chinese.

A hurricane will blow. President Roosevelt announces the intention to use China as a base to invade Japan—the only logical base, but between that announcement of intention and actual planning, there will be another time lag of years. Events will happen and the complex situation will become more complex still, while we say that nothing in the Far East matters until Hitler is defeated. The public realizes now that the cutting off of the Burma Road meant the isolation of China and agrees that London was stupid in not permitting Chinese troops to come into Burma and defend her own vital line, but the public will not admit the stupidity of continuing the present policy of dilly-dallying until either Kunming or Calcutta falls. For Japan was listening when President Roosevelt declared China as the only base for invasion of Japan. Besides, the Japanese know the map of the Orient pretty well, even if the others don't.

Meanwhile, where is the mechanism for concerted Allied action in Asia? General Doolittle bombed Japan in spite of the request of the Government of China that it be delayed a month in order to give time for strengthening the Chinese ground defense of her air bases near Kinhwa. The biggest air base in all Asia with underground concrete hangars was needlessly sacrificed. General Wavell started unilaterally the march toward Akyab without consulting Chungking. Where is the mechanism for concerted action? And why must China's role in 1943 be decided at Casablanca without her representation? And so we must go deeper to the root of the matter.

The Chinese people as a whole are now convinced that the blockade of supplies for China is political and not military. If any doubt in Chinese minds existed, it was completely dispelled by Winston Churchill's speech of March 21, 1943. The situation had clarified, England was feeling confident and strong. On March 17, four days before, the British Prime Minister had made it emphatically clear that "the administration of British colonies"—including India, Burma, the Malay States, the Straits Settlements, and Hong Kong—"must continue to be the sole responsibility of Great Britain." Now he made it plainer than ever that Asia was to be kept down as a system of colonies. The defeat of Hitler was to be the "grand climax of the war," after which only would begin a "new task," the war with Japan and reconquest of Asia. Then and then only, with China kept isolated for years—perhaps till after 1945—would begin the "rescue of China" from the predicament into which the London government had deliberately and according to purpose thrown China by ordering the Burma Road closed a second time. A "rescued" China then would not be a "leading victorious power." In fact, there will be no "leading" or "great victorious" Asiatic "power" at all at the end of the war, so that the nest of White Imperialism will be safe. A "Council of

Asia" will be set up, with "our Dutch Allies" and presumably the French participating. We may be quite sure that at this "Council of Asia" the ruler of the greatest number of Asiatic colonies will naturally have the greatest representation, for the maintenance of "law, justice, and humanity."

Now everything fits into a pattern. The blockade of supplies for China since 1939 can be understood. The closing of the Burma Road and the weakening of China can be understood. The refusal to let China have an air force of her own can be perfectly understood. From the point of view of imperialist strategy, it is superb and masterly. The Empire of Queen Victoria had no better premier and no more devoted servant, with greater sagacity, stronger courage, more far-sighted vision, and a better political genius.

But why this scare about China and about Asia at all? Asia is frightening the Anglo-Saxon powers. By all principles of justice, she need not, but by all principles of power politics, she does frighten them a great deal. The future of Asia at the peace table and after the war seems to me amazingly simple, if we follow the principles of justice. On the other hand, I admit the same problem looks as complicated as that of Middle Europe by all the known principles of power politics. In fact, it can look so complicated that it makes a true partnership of China at the Allied War Council impossible. By bungling, Asian politics can be made complicated enough to look like, and actually become, a nightmare.

Fear, I am told, is one of the greatest driving powers of mankind. Ladies are afraid of mice, diplomats are afraid of birdies, and I am afraid of diplomats. So why shouldn't the diplomats be scared of a mighty Asia? Professor Spykman of Yale, for instance, is terribly afraid of a strong and united China and of a united and strong federated Europe, and I am terribly afraid of Professor Nicholas John Spykman.

What have we got in Asia as we picture the peace ahead of us? Japan has been the upsetting factor. But Japan as a menace will have been eliminated after the war. What then have we got in Asia to settle? There is China, a great pacific power, indoctrinated with principles of human, democratic, peaceful living that are very close to the American temperament. There is India, determined to achieve her freedom, which is nobody's business to interfere with, led by a political party as strong, as truly national in character, and as well organized as the Chinese Kuomintang, and by as wise, capable, patriotic, inspiring, democratic leaders as Chiang Kai-shek. China and India have lived as neighbors without one war in the past four thousand years.

There is no background of racial hatreds, suspicions, wars, or heritage of national antagonisms such as we find in Europe, and the peoples of Asia as a whole are by nature not half as aggressive as the Europeans. Russia will not fight China, nor will China fight Russia. To the Chinese and to the Americans, the future of Asia is simple. There is no problem for the United States, because the United States will let the Philippines go. Other people's jewels don't keep you awake if you have no greed in your heart. No insoluble problems exist if the Christian powers will let Malaya, the Dutch Indies, Siam, Indo-China, Burma, and India go. All of them aspire to self-government, and all of them will give trouble to Europe not when they are masters, but only when they are to be exploited as slaves. The moment you covet any of their territories and their tin and rubber, however, your conscience will irresistibly compel you to station troops there to prevent communal strife and bloodshed, and then all your troubles begin. But whose bloodshed? Will the Javanese or the Indians or the Burmese threaten the United States or England? Will not blood be shed because the westerners will wrangle and fight for their tin and rubber?

On such a simple basis, it is possible to take China into immediate and equal partnership in the war, laying plans together and fighting together and dreaming together for some future better world. Americans want to kill the Japs, and the Chinese want to kill the Japs. America hasn't got a Hong Kong or a Dutch Indies to worry about, and China hasn't got a worry about Indo-China, or Siam, or Burma. China wants to recover her own territory, and does not want others' territory. America wants no territory at all, not even Kulangsu, my childhood home. So let's get together and just kill the Japs as fast as we can, and we don't have to worry if we lick the Japs too soon or defeat Hirohito before we defeat Hitler. Some may want to bomb the Japanese Emperor's palace, and others may not. But these are minor and inconsequential issues that need not make us look beneath the bed before going to sleep at night.

That is the simple picture, a picture of achievable human justice and of a fair prospect of lasting peace in Asia, at least as fair a prospect as there has been in South America since the downfall of the Spanish and Portuguese Empires. For peace is possible in Asia. Peace is possible in North America and South America. Peace is possible in Africa.

Peace is not possible only in Europe. And peace in Asia will become impossible only when Asia assumes the European pattern of balance of power. Of all the five continents of the earth, only Europe has not yet learned to live at peace. Europe is the focus of infection of this earth, and imperialism is the toxin by which it spreads until the whole world is so sick, so sick.

Now for some good old confusion as some of our Allied leaders will have it. If you knew the whole story you would not eat a meal in peace, or sleep a wink at night. If I had to look beneath the bed every night, I wouldn't want to live. But there are people whose minds are otherwise constituted. Not one thug, but possibly three or four, are hiding beneath the diplomats' beds every night. There are great humbugs and they beget little humbugs and they will dance attendance on us all our life, if we will believe the diplomats, until we ourselves get into the diplomats' proper frame of mind.

I have said that facts are always complicated and first principles are the only things we can be certain about. Let's now leave the principles and go after the facts.

The first feeling is one of terrible uncertainty, for we cannot be certain of one knowable fact. What are Russia's intentions? What are China's intentions? As diplomats, we should be prepared for the worst. If China becomes independent and strong, will that not set a bad example for India? Are you so sure China has no imperialist designs? Do not be too sure, if China has an air force of her own, and especially if Japan is completely eliminated. So let's see to it that she will not have even a baby air force of her own when peace comes, and perhaps it is even wise not to knock out Japan completely. What precautions will the white powers have to take in Asia so that the white man will not be completely driven out of the continent? Besides, what will happen if by any mishap we defeat Japan too early, before Hitler is liquidated and before Europe's troubles are solved? Will not American influence predominate in Asia as in North Africa at present? Will not the Dutch Indies and Burma be left very much to themselves, and a little truculent when we settle with Hitler? What will happen to Singapore and to Hong Kong when the Japanese evacuate? . . .

The problem of the colonies is extremely complex. Must one really decide now whether Britain is to keep India, Burma, Malay, Hong Kong? Either "yes" or "no" to this question is very awkward. And if the British must keep their colonies, how are we to force the Dutch to give up theirs? Is it not better for war morale in this War for Freedom if we do not talk about the problem of the colonies until the war is won, when a fighting morale will no longer be necessary?

As a matter of fact, China and England are already heading for conflict. Churchill has made it amply clear and definite that he is not "grovelling," and that the "administration of British colonies" will be the "sole responsibility" of Britain, which is to tell America to keep her hands off. On the other hand, Chiang Kai-shek has made it equally definite and clear that China does not covet others' territory, but wants all her own territory back. These two policies must come to a clash around Hong Kong. China wishes to negotiate on Kowloon, a leased territory opposite Hong Kong, like other leased territories in Shanghai and Tientsin. England refuses to open negotiations. It is thought that dilly-dallying is the best way of treating the problem until it explodes by itself. I have no doubt that if Britain does not return Hong Kong to China, this problem of Hong Kong alone will burst the Peace Conference. I know that the Chinese people are willing to go to war with England over Hong Kong, even if the Chinese government won't. Chinese people have freely expressed the opinion that five million of our soldiers have not died to keep the British in Hong Kong, the booty of the Opium War, and possibly the second brightest jewel in the English Crown.

But really the picture is more complicated than you think. There is Russia, the great bugbear of the democracies. Everything is global nowadays, and we have to think globally. Russia refuses to declare war on Japan, and she knows what she is doing. Japan will be her trump card, and she will not want to play it, but keep it in her hand. What if Russia combines with Hitler and Japan? And what if it is to Russia's advantage to keep Japan in the war while she dictates what she wants to Europe? The thought occurs to us that if Russia can court Japan, why should not some other ally do the same, because after all Hitler is our immediate enemy? . . . Besides, if Russia wants to keep Japan to knock us out, why shouldn't we keep Japan to knock out Russia? Will not the elimination of Japan enhance Russia's power in the East? . . . Will China not double-cross us and negotiate with Japan? No, that is one thing certain at least, thank God! China is honest and dependable, and therefore let's ignore her. . . . She'll have to take what we choose to give her. . . . If Russia would only say something—it keeps one on tenterhooks! Besides, there is the possibility that Russia may combine with China and India and

control the geopoliticians' Eurasian "Heartland" and half of
the world's population. That will be the geopolitician's nightmare come true! Oh, why doesn't Russia say something?

And so like Alice in Wonderland,
the fears grow bigger and
bigger even as the tones
fall lower and lower
until the fears
themselves take
on the shape of
a mouse's tail—
the ugly, filthy
thing. Anyway
look, Russia
is such
a big
power
China
also
is go-
ing
to be
a big
pow-
er
you
can-
not
af-
ford
to
let
Ind-
ia
go
.

.

.

But above all, China herself is the biggest problem. The deeper tendencies of power-political thinking, or statesmanlike foresight according to power politics, already pose an insoluble difficulty. As Professor Spykman warns us, "A modern, vitalized and militarized China of 450,000,000 people is going to be a threat not only to Japan, but also to the position of the Western Powers in the Asiatic Mediterranean." "The preservation of the balance of power will then be necessary not only because of our interest in strategic raw materials [rubber and tin] but because of what unbalanced power in this region could do to the rest of the world." [18] Hence, according to Professor Spykman, in order to set up such a highly desirable balance of power in the Far East, "the United States will have to adopt a similar protective policy toward Japan" as she adopts toward England. However, we are caught at present in the contradictory and illogical position of helping China, our potential enemy, to crush Japan, our potential friend in the Far East. This is confusion worse confounded. Hence we must help China to be strong enough not to be completely knocked out of the war, but not strong enough to stand on her feet after the war and challenge others, while we must crush Japan enough to win the war and not crush her enough so that she cannot revive and recover her power.

If further confusion is desired, I can offer some. Even Professor Spykman's proposal of planning for a half-strong and half-weak China and a half-strong and half-weak Japan does not insure complete security. That these two nations may be so cunningly manipulated that they will keep on fighting each other and exhausting each other for the West's benefit is conceded. It is conceivable, however, that decades from now, Japan and China may one day stupidly wake up to the Professor's clever trick, and realize that they have been set upon one another by the Yale Professor. Nothing so unites two enemies as the knowledge that they have been the common victim of a

---

[18] Nicholas John Spykman, *America's Strategy and World Politics*, p. 469.

third mischievous party. By the time Professor Spykman's high politics prevail in the postwar world, nations will so groan in disillusionment and the spirit of true world co-operation will be such a forgotten thing that economic and political autarchy will be the basic policy of every nation.

The combination of two half-strong nations may nevertheless produce one fully strong power. In fact, writers who insist on Anglo-American domination of the Pacific areas are proceeding upon this theory. They must see to it that no rapprochement between Japan and China will ever be permitted. This, however, can only be done by putting China under military surveillance. On the other hand, China will equally demand putting England under military surveillance because a rapprochement between England and Germany is much more likely than a rapprochement between Japan and China. It is China's business to see that England and Germany do not get together, because every time that happens, a military Germany is resurrected and another World War is produced. China has as much right to demand security in Europe as England has to demand security in the Far East. . . . The Chinese are courteous, but not fools. They do not play power politics, but when others play it they understand it very well.

Such are the necessary and inevitable consequences of thinking on lines suggested by our power-politicians. These are they who pride themselves on "realism" and call us, the people, who believe in the other simple picture of the future of Asia, deluded fools or visionaries. That is what the picture of the future of Asia looks like in terms of power politics, when we transfer our power-political thinking to Asia.

Such may be the "facts" the diplomats are referring to when they say they "know" them, or they may not. One thing is certain, viz., that none of the above "facts" are known or knowable. In the dark, anything that moves may be a mouse's tail. In any case, these are facts which are yet to be produced as consequences of our own acts and created by our own choice.

They are not the objective facts of physical science, and should not share the same scientific prestige. But it is exactly on this type of facts that diplomatic thinking is based, diplomatic fears are generated, and the gall of diplomatic courage is being ruined. It is on the basis of such unknown and unknowable facts that the policy has been established that China must be kept away from any Allied War Council, must be given no air force of her own, and Japan must not be defeated too early, and that a year and a half have elapsed after Pearl Harbor without the Allies coming to a formulated co-ordinated strategic plan for fighting Japan. It is on the basis of such generated fears that we are prevented from fighting together and dreaming together for a better world.

The illiterate shepherds of Asia Minor two thousand years ago heard or related that "Good will toward men" had something to do with "Peace on earth," but the twentieth-century man has advanced scientifically so far that he cannot see the connection, and has descended into confusion. Did Confucius not warn us, "A nation without faith cannot stand"? The same is true of the world.

III. SYMPTOMS

14

PEACE BY POWER

FROM here on, we'll leave the problem of the future of Asia, and delve into the problem of the future of the postwar world. Or rather, we shall never leave it, for the world is one, and nowhere can you escape Asia. We shall probe from the surface techniques of the offered solutions, deeper and deeper down into the sores of men's thinking, until we find the rot within, the despondency of spirit which darkens men's minds in this generation and hangs over it like a shroud, and see, as with an X-ray machine, the leprous growths and misformations which disfigure the spiritual physiognomy of man of this age.

Ultimately, the problem of peace is the problem of the nature of man. The issues of peace and war revolve upon the questions, what man has made of man, and what man can make of man, as Professor Hocking puts it.[19]

Lest I be accused of inventing an imaginary bugaboo with no relation to actual current postwar thinking and planning, I must substantiate the picture.

The material evidence exists in rather uncomfortable abundance. The Clarence Streits and Norman Angells are all not so much for world co-operation as they are against American isolation. Security and freedom and co-operation have been lugged in to make the case for Anglo-American domination of the world picture. The Lionel Gelbers and Stephen King-Halls are unashamed in proclaiming either that this is a "war for power" or that the world police must be an Anglo-American "peace force," while other nationals in that police must swear allegiance to the Commander-in-Chief and therefore to the King of England and the President of the United States. Ely Culbertson revels in the mathematics of an international contract bridge, while Stephen King-Hall does the same with his Anglo-American "peace force." All agree in a regretful tone that some concession must be made to the non-English-speaking powers, so that it may have the appearance of an "international" world order. But there is no hiding the tone of patronizing concession and regret.

I am proud of Harvard postwar thinking, of Professors William Ernest Hocking and Ralph Barton Perry and President Conant. I admire the clear thinking and broad vision of Vice-President Wallace and Wendell Willkie. But for every concrete

---

[19] William Ernest Hocking, *What Man Can Make of Man* (Harper). ‑

proposal for building a postwar world structure genuinely inspired by the conception of a world brotherhood, there are at least two based on power politics and the tacit assumption of Anglo-American domination by force over the entire world.

There is a war about the peace going on now. For the United States and her Allies are now standing at the crossroads: one leading to a sound and stable world order based on equality and co-operation of all nations, and the other leading to world mastery or world domination through sheer military force by America in the exclusive company of Britain. These two tendencies are basic and contradictory, but on the surface at least world mastery must be passed off as world co-operation or world federation, and so the two tend constantly to merge and work for the progress and happiness of mankind.

Only once in a while do we find a Lionel Gelber who comes out definitely for a "war for power": *"In reality the war is one for power—for power of the Democracies before it is a power for democracy itself."* [20] Mr. Gelber is for the Versailles Treaty—"No new Versailles? No new Versailles for whom?" He is for maintenance of the status quo, and regrets that even Sumner Welles joins in the "vilification" of the status quo. He is even for the future of humanity "belonging" to the two Anglo-Saxon powers: "What must settle the future of mankind is to whom it belongs and how it is used. In the hands of the west, even though they falter, power will be employed in one fashion; in German hands, it will be employed in another." This contrast so pleases him that he exclaims, ". . . none but the frivolous still can wonder what the war is all about." Finally Mr. Gelber pretends not to understand the "paradox," which he regards as exceptionally "odd," which is "the tacit assumption by friend and foe alike that to call it a struggle between rival imperialisms is to belittle the Allied cause. . . . It all depends upon whose imperialism you are talking about," he shouts,

---

[20] For this and following quotations, see Lionel Gelber: *Peace by Power*, pp. 10, 58-60, 68, 130, 140.

gently reminding his readers that while an Italian imperialism "would be execrable, *the reinforcement of American imperialism . . . will be acclaimed by all level-headed, free men everywhere.*" I thought when he wrote the word "level-headed," it was sufficient recommendation of his point of view; the juxtaposition of "free men" there seems at the least tautological, for by definition "free men everywhere" would acclaim imperialism anyway.

Mr. Gelber, I suspect, is young, or he is inspired; other mature heads are more cautious. Concessions are made, and will be made, for the participation of powers other than the United States and Britain in the world government—and this always in a condescending tone. On this most agree. Mr. Stephen King-Hall is more circumscribed in explaining the existence of an Anglo-American "peace force":

> The British and American Governments would not wish to deny to any power of goodwill the privilege of partaking in the chastisement of the aggressor. All they intend to do is to make themselves responsible for the maintenance of a force large enough and efficient enough in all circumstances to do the job, with or without assistance.[21]

Professor Spykman speaks with scholarly caution in words, if he is without scholarly caution in thoughts, on the hegemony of England and America:

> Both in England and in the United States, there is talk of a world order based on American-British hegemony. The theme appears in several variations, from Mr. Streit's Anglo-American union to looser forms of alliance and entente. The Anglo-American Federalists present their program as a first stage in the creation of a world federa-

---

[21] Stephen King-Hall: *Total Victory*, p. 219.

tion and they concede that other states, upon certificate of good behavior, will eventually be permitted to join. The fact remains, however, that in the meantime the union is expected to function as a hegemony.[22]

Professor Spykman was not the first enlightened modern to think of this hegemony-within-federation idea; the Delian Confederacy under Pericles carried it out two thousand years ago, to the complete destruction of all Greece.

But this is getting into tiresome arguments on generalities, which level-headed men hate. Let's have some wizard figures. Figures cleanse the air of our thought, for we are told they make our thinking mathematical and exact, and that is after all what a college education is for. The editor of the famous King-Hall *News Letters* goes to the trouble of working out some clear and awe-inspiring figures for us. Article 3 of "The Anglo-American Proclamation to Mankind," to be issued by the President of the United States and the English King reads:

> Therefore the President and the King have undertaken to establish a joint British-American Fleet and Air Force. The strength of the Fleet will be in all respects three times that of the next largest fleet afloat at any given moment and not less than twice as strong as any combination of any other three forces.

Article 4 reads:

> The strength of the Air Force will be not less than four times as great in all respects as the next largest air force and twice as strong as any possible combination of two other air forces.

Article 7 reads:

> Eighty per cent of the personnel of the British-American

[22] Nicholas John Spykman: *America's Strategy in World Politics*, pp. 458-459.

Fleet and Air Force will be British and American citizens. Foreign subjects shall be eligible to enlist . . . up to a total of 20 per cent of the whole establishment of each force. Foreign subjects desirous of serving in the Peace Force will be required to take an oath of loyalty to the Commander-in-Chief of the branch of the Peace Force in which they enlist.[23]

Soul of Pericles again!

Suppose the modern Sparta would not agree? Mr. King-Hall has a ready answer, which seems as simple as Hitler's own arithmetic.

> Provided the American and British Governments make it clear that whatever those countries decide to do, the English-speaking peoples intend, as it were, "to double the number first thought of," we doubt whether the other great Powers would take up the challenge in an armaments race in which they were bound to be defeated.

Tell that to the United States Congress; tell it to the Marines! The cutting up of the world between "English-speaking peoples" and "non-English-speaking peoples" is now perfect. God always works with opposites, like electrons and protons. The world cannot be thoroughly annihilated except by dividing it into two big armed camps. Neither Germans, nor Frenchmen, nor Italians, nor Spaniards, nor Swedes, nor Czechs, nor Poles, nor Russians, nor Chinese, nor Indians, nor Turks happen to speak English. What a thought! What obscenity of mind!

We cannot escape history, nor can we learn from history.

---

[23] Stephen King-Hall, *Total Victory*, p. 215.

15

A PHILOSOPHY OF PEACE

THAT grown-up men today, well educated and well informed, should talk and think in such simple-minded fashion is alarming. Perhaps God cuts short the span of animal and plant life in order that the world may be perpetually young. Reproduction is merely God's method of perpetual rejuvenation of the species. My mind is young yet in spite of my years—will someone answer for me the puzzling question: How can there be a pile of dry gunpowder, a well-connected fuse, a box of burning matches near by, and no explosion? It is rather the Sphinx that is asking that question, and when anyone answers it she will jump into the sea. I am willing to be the hostage for it. . . .

The question which we must solve once for all, by some sort of new philosophy of peace, which we may not leave unsolved, is really this: does Force work? All over the world men and women should ponder this question. If Force is thoroughgoing, it arouses resentment and hatred in human beings to whom it is applied and corrupts the human beings who apply it: it therefore invites more use of Force and must end in sheer brutality, as Nazi Germany has found out. If Force is not thoroughgoing, does it not, according to the doctrine of Force, immediately show signs of "weakness" which leaves room for the politics of appeasement, cajolery, yielding, compromise, pacifying measures, buying loyalty from neutral powers in order to draw these into its own orbit of power—in other words, does it not imply the alternate use of firmness and concession, which can be equally fatal in the re-arming of subject nations as in the case of resurrected Germany after Versailles? Be firm to the end and you hang yourself; be not firm to the end, and you also hang yourself. The first variation in the use of Force is destroying Japan and Germany. The second variation destroyed the League of Nations and Ancient Greece.

Who will make plain to the world the law of the spirit, and demonstrate that Force generates Coercion, Coercion generates Fear, and Fear generates Hatred, as definitely and as accurately as one billiard ball sends another rolling? Who will write a philosophy and psychology of Force and its reactions and determine their characteristics? Who will be the consummate fatalist to tell the world in plain, convincing, forceful terms that actions generate emotions and emotions in turn generate actions, that the fruit of Force is Fear and Hatred, that thoroughgoing Force generates Fear and Hatred and unthoroughgoing Force generates Hatred without Fear? Who will say, even as in a classroom in physics, that the greater the Force, the greater the Hatred, and that the greatest Force is the most hated of all? And who will say, as clearly as the prophets of the sky say that a thunderclap presages a storm, that Force is inevitably followed by Hatred, and Hatred is followed by Revenge? For Hatred divides, and the structure of power must sooner or later fall.

In ignorance of such simple and self-evident moral laws, Pericles alternately threatened by force and cajoled by oratory the other Greek states. And after his death, Cleon the leather merchant, Eucrates the rope-seller, and Hyperbolus the lampmaker babbled. They were all good democrats and Cleon was a good general. It was left only for the insolent public idol, Alcibiades, to complete the suicide of Greece.

But such laws, being the laws of God, are manifest to the mind of the simple man, requiring no proof. Therefore, he who would be strong within must guard against the use of power, for only then is he safe from corruption within and hatred without. And only he who is free from corruption within and hatred without can be strong eternally. Laotse says, "For love is

victorious in attack and invulnerable in defense. Heaven arms
with love those it would not see destroyed." Therefore he says:

Of all things, soldiers are instruments of evil,
    Hated by men.
Therefore the religious man avoids them.

Soldiers are weapons of evil;
    They are not the weapons of the gentleman.
When the use of soldiers cannot be helped,
    The best policy is calm restraint.

Even in victory, there is no beauty,
And who calls it beautiful
    Is one who delights in slaughter.
He who delights in slaughter
    Will not succeed in his ambition to rule the world.
The slaying of multitudes should be mourned
        with sorrow.
A victory should be celebrated with the Funeral Rite.[24]

Those who love America and England and wish them to be
strong forever must read Laotse again and again, for they will
gain thereby the secret of immortal strength, exempt from corruption within and invulnerable from attack without. Let
America be great, even as the great river of life:

The Great Tao flows everywhere,
    (Like a flood) it may go left or right.
The myriad things derive their life from it,
    And it does not deny them.
When its work is accomplished,
    It does not take possession.

[24] For this and following quotations see *Wisdom of China and India*, pp. 600-602,
617, 622.

It clothes and feeds the myriad things,
  Yet does not claim them as its own . . .
Because to the end it does not claim greatness,
  Its greatness is achieved.

How did the great rivers and seas become the Lords
    of the Ravines?
By being good at keeping low.
That was how they became the Lords of the Ravines.

Therefore in order to be the chief among the people,
  One must speak like their inferiors.
In order to be foremost among the people,
  One must walk behind them.
Thus it is that the sage stays above,
  And the people do not feel his weight;
Walks in front,
  And the people do not wish him harm.
Then the people of the world are glad to uphold
    him forever.
Because he does not contend,
No one in the world can contend against him.

I am not worried lest America may not be able to assert a
leadership of force and power; I am worried lest she may. I
am concerned to see America assume a moral leadership, a
leadership of humility, so that the world may pay her glad
homage and uphold her forever. Like the great river that nour-
ishes life along its valley, she shall by the exuberance and
richness of her life be a blessing upon the peoples of the earth.
She shall stay above, and the world shall not feel her weight;
she shall walk in front and no one will wish her harm. For
she shall then lead in kindness and unselfishness and justice
and by that secret of unused power bring a new era of brotherhood to mankind. No one can dethrone her because of her

power for goodness, and no one can take away from her, because she does not take possession. She shall not contend, and no one in the world can contend against her, and because she takes no credit, the credit can never be taken away from her. This is my Dream America. Will it come true?

Man has done it before. Abraham Lincoln did it. George Washington did it. In a world of evil chaos, great men have stood up and with the strength of their goodness and their simplicity and the innocence of youth proclaimed that the good in men can outweigh the evil, and they have acted upon that assumption. For there are periods in history when the Good Fairy ruled, while others were ruled by the Wicked Fairy. Sometimes the good influence was in the air, and men and women submerged their selfishness and felt as on the dawn of another era, and the golden horizon was visible, when faith caught their vision and warmed their hearts and strengthened them. Then the good impulses of men prevailed. And there were other periods, of chaos and cynicism and despair, when the petty spirits of the age prevailed. Then faith sounded hollow, and idealism bowed its head in shame and seemed strangely out of place. Such periods presaged the ruin of a regime or a culture. The moral strength to lift oneself to a higher plane than mankind's predecessors was not there because the moral fibers had become flabby and weakened by a shallow cynicism. Then darkness fell. And between the two, the difference was that between Faith and Despair.

But a spiritual softening of tone is necessary for this Age, when men's minds are made in the image of steel. The harshness must go off, its crudities must be purged and purified as in a crucible, and a mellower way of thinking and reasoning must prevail. The leaven of the Sermon on the Mount has softened man's ways in social living in the Christian world; it is the only thing that holds the society of western men together whether in the country or the town, and softens the hardness of aggressive men. Somehow the Bible at times still terrifies the thug. But Christianity has no influence over world politics. There are plenty of raw lumps in the dough of Christendom, though it has been mixed for two thousand years with the leaven of Jesus. A good housewife would perhaps add a pinch of Laotse and hasten the process.

For man's spirit lives in a high nervous tension because arterio-sclerosis has set in. The high-pressured march and conflict of forces has the terrific power of steam. The blast furnace roars, molten, white-hot, gleaming, liquid steel flows over and splatters about, and amidst the steady hum of booming, buzzing, clicking and clanking machines, giant iron crab-pincers snap and clang, huge drums slide and roll and swing overhead, and the slightest false step may mean the loss of an arm or a life. Metal, metal, metal—liquid, glowing, hardening, blackening metal. In the roaring and clangor before the blast furnace, man tries to think, furiously, at high temperature, and his thoughts partake of the metallic ring, while he is afraid of himself and of his power. A little reading of Laotse will do him good and take the hardness out of his heart and the glint out of his eyes.

> When man is born, he is tender and weak;
>   At death, he is hard and stiff.
> When the things and plants are alive, they are soft
>   and supple;
>   When they are dead, they are brittle and dry.
> Therefore hardness and stiffness are the
>   companions of death,
> And softness and gentleness are the companions
>   of life.
>
> Therefore when an army is headstrong, it
>   will lose in battle.
> When a tree is hard, it will be cut down.
> The big and strong belong underneath.
> The gentle and weak belong at the top.

16

PEACE BY POINT RATIONS

LET'S go back to the wizard of figures, Ely Culbertson. Perhaps Euclid and Pythagoras can help us and with their figures establish a peace for us. What charms me in Culbertson's plan is his precise mathematical reasoning and the matching of a clear mind against big problems. The question is what can be done with sheer mathematics, with a peace-point-ration system.

It is fair to caution the reader against mixing up Mr. Culbertson with those power politicians. He has studied mass psychology, but he is not a professor of psychology, nor is he a politician; he is an unpretentious thinking man like you and me, and a man of uncommon intelligence and clear thinking. If Euclid or Pythagoras could save us, Culbertson will. Moreover, Mr. Culbertson has a lot of common sense. He is able to see the inherent danger of international coercion and resentment arising from the existence of an international police force that serves as the cloak of sectional, national domination, the greatest danger of all schemes for a police force, and he is concentrating his thinking on the elimination of that psychological danger. We feel here a sense of fairness and good will to start with. His presentation of dilemmas, remedies, and comments is clear, lucid, and precise. That is why I am discussing it as one of the most attractive schemes of world co-operation. Besides, playing a game of international bridge is fun: it exercises the brains.[25]

We are not going into a full examination of the "World Federation Plan." It has a "World Armament Trust," a "World President," "World Trustees," "World Judges," and "World

[25] Ely Culbertson, *The World Federation Plan* (The World Federation, Inc.). Distributed by Garden City Publishing Co.

Senators." It has a "World Constitution" and plans for three time periods: the "War Period," the "Armistice Period," and the "Postwar Period," the first two periods being under the "Provisional Government." It has a "World Territorial Table," dividing the world into eleven "Regional Federations," including "sovereign two-way states" (like Switzerland, Danzig) and "Autonomous Regional Federations" (the Indian and the Malaysian).

But the most distinctive feature of the plan is the "Quota Force Principle" which is mathematics. Each Regional Federation would have a "National Contingent," and there would be an additional "Collective Quota," the "Mobile Corps," owned by all the member Regional Federations, which is like a "joker," or better, like the "widow" at poker, that all hands can count as their own.

The dilemma that Mr. Culbertson is trying to solve is how to harmonize the existence of the "World Police" with national sovereignty. He solves it by the interesting formula that while the national contingents are all parts of the "World Police" in time of war, in time of peace each is a national force policing its own territory, and no foreign national contingent may step into its territory. Furthermore, since these "National Contingents" form a "World Police" by pooling their strength, each contingent is adequate for defense of its own territory, and none is adequate for attacking others with any chance of success.

THE QUOTA PRINCIPLE OF WORLD POLICE

Quota	National Contingent of Initiating State	Where Stationed	Regional Federation Represented
20%	United States	United States; Leased Bases in Western Hemisphere Islands and in Malaysian Federation	American
15%	British (including English-speaking Dominions)	British Empire; leased Bases in Indian Federation	British

THE QUOTA PRINCIPLE OF WORLD POLICE—*Cont.*

Quota	National Contingent of Initiating State	Where Stationed	Regional Federation Represented
15%	Russian	U. S. S. R.	Russian
4%	French	France	Latin-European (Latin)
4%	German	Germany	Northern European (Germanic)
4%	Polish	Poland	Middle European
4%	Turkish	Turkey	Middle Eastern
4%	Chinese	China	Chinese
4%	Indian (provisionally selected under British Command)	India	Indian
2%	Malaysian (provisionally selected under American Command)	Malaysian Federation	Malaysian
2%	Japanese	Japan	Japanese
	Mobile Corps		
22%	All member-states not listed above (non-initiating states)	Two-way states and strategic islands owned by the World Federation	All the member Regional Federations (Collective quota)

ILLUSTRATIVE TABLE OF THE QUOTA FORCE PRINCIPLE

Initiating State	Quota	National Troops	Planes	Tanks	Battleships or Aircraft Carriers
United States	20%	400,000	10,000	20,000	20
Britain	15%	300,000	7,500	15,000	15
Russia	15%	300,000	7,500	15,000	15
Germany	4%	80,000	2,000	4,000	4
France	4%	80,000	2,000	4,000	4
Poland	4%	80,000	2,000	4,000	4
Turkey	4%	80,000	2,000	4,000	4
China	4%	80,000	2,000	4,000	4
India	4%	80,000	2,000	4,000	4
Malaysia	2%	40,000	1,000	2,000	2
Japan	2%	40,000	1,000	2,000	2
Mobile Corps .... (Collective Quota)	22%	440,000	11,000	22,000	22
Total	100%	2,000,000	50,000	100,000	100

The cards being dealt out, let's sit down to play the international contract bridge game. The merit of this mathematical distribution of forces, according to its author, is the following:

> The quota mechanism not only eliminates military dictatorships and wars between single nations; it eliminates wars between alliances or coalitions of nations. On the basis of the Quota Force Principle, it is impossible to point out any politically conceivable combination of nations which could conduct a war of aggression against the remaining nations of the World Federation without being decisively outnumbered.
>
> Let us assume the most powerful (although the least likely) combination of nations some years after the World Federation is founded: The United States, Great Britain, and Germany decide to rebel against the World Federation and to conquer the World. Without the Quota Force Principle, there is no question but that this coalition of powers could easily dominate the world. With the Quota Force Principle, the joint Quota of these three nations would be only 39%. Against them there would be lined up Armored Forces of planes, tanks, and warships totaling 61%, of which 22%, the Mobile Corps, would be the Shock Troops. Before England and Germany (19%) would have time to develop their industrial potential into a military potential, they would be overwhelmed, isolating the United States with its 20%.
>
> Let us reverse the situation and assume a communist-dominated Europe and Asia, in revolt against the World Federation and the Anglo-Americans. Without the World Federation, a Communist Japan, China, Poland, Russia, Germany, and France, lined up against the Anglo-Americans, would automatically result in a Third World War. With the World Federation, the Quotas of the rebel communist nations would total only 33% against the 67%

total of the Mobile Corps, the Anglo-Americans, and the
other Contingents of the World Police.

In other words, no one will have a grand slam. The cards
are, in fact, so dealt out that no one will bid at all. If mathematics will give us a peace, this plan will do so. If the cat
can be belled, if Russia will accept the cards dealt out to her,
if no card-player nods, if all the players are equally skillful,
or equally reckless, or equally cautious, or equally honest, or
equally good at making passes to neighbors or slipping cards
from their sleeves, above all, if all the players love and trust
one another, there should be no bid and no play at all. If there
are no upsetting factors like different national psychologies,
national ambitions, and cultural traditions, if eternal vigilance
can be kept up, if the "World Government" is able to act
promptly and despatch the "Mobile Corps" instantly, if it will
not appoint another Lytton Commission to take a year to make
a report for the purpose of being filed, if it is easy to define
"aggression" and "defense," if there is not the question of industrial potentials, if there is no question of commercial avia-
tion, if all people are equally aggressive or equally satisfied
with what they have, if no nation secretly rearms or openly
defies and denounces the quota system, if the different "National Contingents" and the "Mobile Corps" are equidistant
from the point of conflict, if there are no questions of sea and
land transportation to distant continents, and if all are available at a moment's notice, if no state member hesitates or
remains neutral at the call of duty, if there are, for instance,
no internal factions in Czechoslovakia or between Czechoslovakia and Poland when Russia or Germany rebels, if above all,
no single nation dominates the "World Government," if the
"World Judges" do not take orders from the big powers, if
the "World Senate" could not be captured from within, if the
big powers would refrain from manipulating the "World
Government" into their private machine as they did with the

League of Nations, if there are no problems of corruption and failing enthusiasm and division of mind and even change of mind among the powers, if there is no selfish disposition of the "Mobile Corps," if there is no underhanded manipulation and control of important strategic material, if there is no progress in chemical industry, no development of new weapons undefined, if there is a guarantee that national sentiments in the different states will not change, if there is no selfish isolationism, if economic autocracy does not set in in any one state, if there is indeed justice, and if there is no racial discrimination, then we shall indeed have a fair prospect of peace by this plan. In other words, if this is a mechanical game and the cards are cards, and not quarrelsome, fickle-minded, and always progressing human beings, the game will never be played and the cards will remain as they are dealt out at the beginning. Then, thank Heaven, we shall have no war!

We might conveniently take this quota table for the study of how complicated psychological factors underlie plain arithmetic. There is no question that the quota table will be acceptable to the United States army and navy experts, and fairly acceptable to British experts. But why should Russia, with a greater territory and bigger population, accept a lower quota than the United States, particularly in view of the traditional combination of England and America, and the English control of the Indian Federation and the American control of the Malaysian Federation? Who will bell the Russian cat?

It is clear that raising the common "collective quota" of the international "Mobile Corps" and lowering the percentage of the national contingents of the "Big Powers" would accomplish every purpose Mr. Culbertson desires more surely and more effectively than the low collective quota and high quotas for certain particular powers in sharp contrast to the rest of the nations. Equal quotas for the Regional Federations and a high common collective quota for all would seem to represent the principle of international justice and sincerity, and create greater confidence. It would be a simple idea to give that collective quota 50 per cent, and then no matter what the combinations of "rebellious" "National Contingents" are, they would still be less than the collective quota obeying the command of the "World Government," unless the whole world revolts against the "World Government," which is an absurdity. Even a 32-34 per cent for the collective quota would secure a readier approval, on either of the following formulas:

(A) Collective Quota 34%
    11 National Contingents
    (averaging 6% each) 66%

(B) Collective Quota 32%
    Russia, China, Britain, and U. S.
    (10% each) 40%
    7 other Contingents
    (averaging 4% each) 28%

Under the "B" plan, a U. S.-Britain combination or a Russia-China combination would give only 20 per cent as against the Collective Quota of 34 per cent, or against 80 per cent of the World Police.

Why is this not suggested? And here we come at once to the root of the matter, which is psychological. *For the acceptance of America and Great Britain the principle is consent, and for the acceptance of Russia the principle is coercion.* "It would have been desirable, perhaps, to lower the American and British quotas even further. But in that event, it is unlikely that the majority of the British Parliament would approve it, and highly improbable that two-thirds of the American Senate would vote for such a risky commitment." But why "risky," particularly if there is a bigger collective quota? How about the risky commitment for Russia? We read:

It is possible that Russia, mindful of her bitter pre-war experiences with the capitalistic countries and suspicious of their future intentions, might adopt a policy of total isolation until convinced that the World Federation is designed for her benefit as well as for that of other nations . . . there could be no objection on Russia's part if the World Federation should increase its own total armed strength, parallel to Russian increases, so as to maintain the Quota Force Principle.

We are back in the same rut again, the rut of armament race, which is a risky matter, and of political coercion, which is still riskier.

And here we receive a strong and clear hint from Sir Norman Angell that Anglo-American conduct during the peace as during the war will be along the line of "unilateral" action. Clarence Streit and all other advocates of Anglo-American union or domination think in exactly the same way: *The other nations may take it or leave it, the World Government will not be based on consent of the world.* For Sir Norman Angell said in his New York Town Hall speech of March 11, 1943:

> Note this, the American elder statesmen in adopting the Monroe Doctrine did not proceed first of all by drawing up an elaborate Pan-American Constitution. They did not even get in touch with the Latin-American Republics. *The Declaration was unilateral. This, it seems to me, is a pregnant hint for today.*[26]

Sir Norman Angell is really getting more and more exasperated.

But why the higher quota for the big powers and a low quota for the other powers? Here we run into a series of inverted reasonings. Because, Mr. Culbertson says, the small

---

[26] As reported in the *New York Times*, March 12, 1943.

powers would combine and attack the big powers! Where in history have the small nations ever had the wit to combine in defense, much less in attack? Does not history teach the exact reverse? Was it Norway or Switzerland or Denmark that threatened world peace? But we read:

> The ideal distribution of the World Police might seem to be the assignment of an equal Quota to each of the eleven Regional Federations. But this would be unrealistic. In computing the Quotas one must keep in mind not only the factors of territory and industrial capacity, but the psycho-political factor as well. If each Region had an equal Quota of the World's Armed Forces, then the poorer regions (which are in great majority) might seek to combine for an attack against the few prosperous ones.

It is the old story of Finland threatening the security of Russia. Why not seek safety in a bigger "Collective Quota" and have a little more confidence in the "World Government"? It would seem that the psycho-political principle should operate against nations which have a historical record of aggressiveness rather than against the historically peace-loving small nations.

In the case of China, the inverted reasoning is even more apparent. I know Mr. Culbertson is well disposed toward China. The inverted reasoning he employs—one set of reasoning for China, another for America and Great Britain—is purely unconscious and profoundly human. A *Lebensraum* of continental dimensions is the reason for a higher quota in the case of the United States, Britain, and Russia; the same fact is adduced as the reason for denying it to China. And why? *Because China "threatens" the other powers.* We read:

> In the deeper sense of future reality, it is perhaps best for the peace of the world that the United States, Britain

and Russia should be the ones with a preponderance of Quota strength. Each has a *lebensraum* of continental dimensions, the economy of each is inwardly, not outwardly, expanding [*sic!*]. Each is threatened by powerful rivals— rump super-states like Germany, which lacks *lebensraum,* or embryonic super-states like China, which lacks technology.

So the story is that, China, which lacks technology (or war potential) is threatening either Russia or the United States which have it!

Mr. Culbertson makes it quite clear that the size of China's population, a territory easy to defend, and a homogeneous population are the reasons for China's being assigned 4 per cent, while the same factors are the reasons for Russia and the United States being give 15 to 20 per cent. Mr. Culbertson admits the "seeming injustice," which he "explains" as follows:

> In the case of China, it would seem that this heroic nation of five hundred million people should be entitled to more than 4%. Actually, the very size of her population is the main reason for China's relatively low Quota. China has not only a very low industrial capacity and territory which is fairly easy to defend, but she possesses an enormous homogeneous population. She will have trained forces for internal policing at least four times the size of that of the United States. Although such a police force will have no heavy weapons, it will be *in effect,* a supporting infantry. Hence her Quota of 4%.[27]

I don't follow you, Mr. Culbertson.

---

[27] The last sentence, "Hence her Quota of 4%," appearing in the original mimeographed copy has been struck out in the printed and revised edition. This is interesting. It was meant to clinch an argument, but Mr. Culbertson must have felt that instead of clinching the argument, it weakened it.

The psychological reason is deeper than that. Mr. Culbertson really would not want China to lay herself open to the suspicion of imperialism and invite the fear of the world. It is only later that we read the real reason, as suggested in a world without the "Quota Force Principle."

> Furthermore, the World Federation enables China to develop industrially *without exciting the fears of other great nations.* Without the World Federation, power-politics might dictate that other nations should sooner or later strike at China, to prevent her five hundred million people from becoming too powerful industrially and therefore militarily.

But even within the World Federation, the same dilemma really exists: either strangle China industrially or allow her to develop until she will demand a revision of the quota for equality with the other nations, and this demand for revision will have to be kept down by coercion at the point of the bayonet, or by stubborn manipulation of the "World Government." It will be the story of the "5:5:3," in altered forms—the basis of the present war with Japan. Such complications always arise when we get "realistic" and forsake the principle of equality.

That China may be coerced into acceptance or remain outside is another matter. If she does accept 4 per cent, it will not be because of coercion, but because of the old rogue's Laotsean philosophy of the wisdom of appearing foolish, the advantage of lying low, the strength of gentility, and the victory that comes from not inviting the fear of the world. I am sure of it. The fear is that the younger nations will not live by the wisdom of avoiding fear and hatred and ruin by insolence. "To pretend to be a damn fool" is such a common phrase in Chinese that I constantly forget it isn't an English idiom. Who but a Chinese scholar would call himself "Guard Stupidity" or

"Embrace Folly"? *But I know eventually it is white insolence that will ruin any world co-operation.*

No, the problem of peace is not a problem of mathematics, but a problem of the psychology of the big powers. The problem of world peace is no more a problem of mathematics than the problem of conducting a campaign is the problem of disposition of troops and topography; very often, given the troops and the tanks, it is only the problem of the commanding general's personality, his mind, his courage, his quick decision, his capacity to get along with his officers, and his attitude toward his superiors, his rivals, and his enemy.

Battles have been lost because the general was thinking of his mistress in the enemy camp, and peace has been lost because the Lavals were busily traveling to Berlin and Rome. And while the conception of power politics remains what it is and the statesmen of the leading powers still sit in their moronic complacency, with no mental comprehension of how the war arose and what it is being fought for, except certain colonial possessions and the status quo, peace will forever remain an elusive hope and the blood of our children and grandchildren must flow.

May I suggest a simple solution? May I claim and demonstrate that peace has been possible? May I substantiate it by history and point out that peace has not been an empty dream, but a reality, an accomplished historic fact, in many quarters of this earth? Without a convention, and without quotas, peace has already been achieved between Canada and the United States. Without a convention, or federation, or the "Quota Force Principle," peace has been achieved in the continent of South America already. And may I also suggest that there was peace in Asia in the centuries preceding the coming of the white man? That there has been peace in Tahiti and Bali and the Samoan Islands? Peace, too, in Greenland and Iceland.

And may I point out why? There is peace in South America and in the Caribbean Sea because the Spanish and Portuguese

Empires have collapsed. There have been civil wars, but we are not interested in local civil wars; we are speaking of the large patterns of world history. There will be peace in the world only when the English, French, and Dutch Empires collapse. I know this war is not big enough to reverse the process and wipe out the Empires, and I hope World War III will do it. If the imperialist powers will not worry overmuch about the "capacity for self-government" of the Filipinos, the Javanese, the Indians, and Burmese, there will be peace, too, in the Philippines, the Dutch Indies, India, and Burma. But if they do not stop worrying overmuch about the capacity for self-government of the colonies, wars will continue to be fought in the home countries themselves.

Civil wars are necessary in a nation until an equilibrium is restored. Revolts against empires are necessary until the invader is driven out. The only stable equilibrium in the world is the equilibrium of equality. Only when such equilibrium is reached can we have peace. Small countries have the right to fight, perhaps to settle an old boundary dispute. Big countries have no right to fight, ever, because when they fight they involve the whole world. When small countries fight, it is at least their own business; when the big powers fight, it is always because they want to interfere with someone else's business. Small countries do not fight, because they always have enough territory. Big countries fight, because curiously what they have is never enough—they need *Lebensraum*. Finally, all countries, whether big or small, do not fight because they are contented, and all countries, whether big or small, fight because they are discontented. As Laotse says, "There is no greater curse than the lack of contentment, no greater sin than the desire for possession. Therefore he who is contented with contentment shall be always content."

And so Mr. Culbertson is putting the cart before the horse when he puts arithmetic before psychology. Of all the fifty or sixty nations in the world, only three or four big powers are upsetting the peace of the world. These powers have run over this earth, kicking down people's fences in bad temper and worse manners, robbing them of their liberty and independence, and taking possession of their goods—and have then fought wars among themselves for these goods. First they fought among themselves, and then they called upon the entire world to fight for them to keep what they have. This makes little sense, and it makes still less sense to say that we can have peace only by giving greater power to the big powers and disarming the small powers, on the plea that the small powers may combine to attack them!

Big Powers, at least behave as if you were not scared! But now we suddenly hear about policing the world, as if the Greenlanders and Samoans and Formosans and Burmese were threatening the world peace, while the big powers don their uniforms, strutting about to club the small powers on their heads with a baton if they do not behave. It would seem that we could well police the big powers for a while and leave the poor Samoans and Balinese and Eskimos alone. But, no, we cannot disarm the big powers, because the big powers will not be disarmed, after having so heroically fought and triumphed in this war. Very well, then, let's have wars eternally. The first thing we know the police will start shooting among themselves and scare us poor humble neighbors out of our wits.

17

THE SCIENCE OF THE BLOODY EARTH

NO, the root of war lies deeper. Mr. Culbertson is the opposite of the power politicians. He is on our side. Those on the other side are legion, and their sores are touchy. Probe gently, for it hurts and it is a case requiring the greatest surgical skill. "He who has an ugly disease shuns the doctor," says a Chinese proverb. The leprous growths are many and spread in all directions, for power politics is an old, old disease, and we shall not do our job until we have slashed open the patient and cut out the toxin-secreting tumors of Naturalism, Determinism, and Despair.

And while we are approaching the pseudo-scientific ground of geopolitics, which speaks of states as "organisms," let us remember that disease is also an organism. Disease fights to survive as much as life itself. It feeds upon the blood and tissues of the patient and fights hard to maintain its ground. It buries itself in the body, builds itself a fortress, and fights back. So has the disease of power-politics built itself a beautiful mansion called the Hall of Geopolitics, before whose portals stands the statue of a naked lady, Science, stolen from the Natural Museum, and on whose frieze stand the sacrilegeous inscriptions of Bacon, Linnaeus, Leibnitz, Humboldt, Hegel, Wagner, and Darwin. It has shining corridors and a bright library and a sea of archives in well-numbered dossiers, and clean, white-tiled latrines. For anything worthy of the name of science now has clean, white-tiled latrines. How Darwin and Linnaeus and Humboldt ever became scientists and discovered things without these latrines is still one of the unsolved mysteries of modern scientific history.

We can now well let alone the special champions of Anglo-American dominion, for there is sufficient material on every hand, and one does not usually try to show a whole desert, after showing a corner of it. Rather should we hurry our steps and examine where the deep-rooted sores of our spirit lie, and diligently search until we have found the source of infection. We may conveniently take geopolitics as such an affection of the spirit; we shall turn it about until we see what makes modern men think the way we do.

For geopolitics is, after all, a kind of philosophy and *Weltan-*

schauung, a thing of the mind, where Nazi scholars and anti-Nazi scholars meet and shake hands in profound admiration of one another. It is out of such minds, out of the character of modern scholarship, that modern power politics grows, flourishes, and has its being. In Professor Nicholas John Spykman we have the foremost geopolitician in America today and therefore a fair specimen, not of all college minds, but of some of them, where the dehumanization of scholarship has reached the ultimate process, and science and the conscience of man part ways.

Professor Spykman is frankly a serious exponent of world power politics. The subtitle of *America's Strategy in World Politics* is "The United States and the Balance of Power." He believes profoundly in power politics and exhibits all its symptoms. He holds that:

> Basically, the new order will not differ from the old, and international society will continue to operate with the same power patterns. It will be a world of power politics in which the interests of the United States will continue to demand the preservation of the balance of power in Europe and Asia.[28]

Consequently, he is for an Anglo-American-Japanese hegemony of the world. He is against unity in Europe, by either federation or dominion by one power, for:

> A federal Europe would constitute an agglomeration of force that would completely alter our significance as an Atlantic power and greatly weaken our position in the Western Europe. *If the peace objective of the United States is the creation of a United Europe, we are fighting on the*

---

[28] *America's Strategy in World Politics,* p. 461. For following quotations, see pp. 460, 466, 470.

wrong side. All-out aid to Mr. Hitler would be the quickest way to achieve an integrated trans-Atlantic zone.

In other words, we are fighting really to preserve a disunited Europe. We are fighting on the right side because we are fighting against that unity and integration of Europe, and we are helping the English to fight for no other reason than to keep Europe embroiled so that the United States may be a more "significant" Atlantic power. Therefore, he is for American hegemony in Asia, Europe, and America. And in order to do this, the United States must "continue the struggle" until she has annihilated the power of Russia and China, after defeating Germany and Japan.[29] To accomplish all this and keep it up, however, she must restore power to Germany and Japan and plan the ruin of Russia and China. "Washington might become convinced of the British argument that asks for the continued existence of a powerful Germany." "If the balance of power in the Far East is to be preserved, the United States will have to adopt a similar protective policy toward Japan [as toward England]. The present inconsistency in American policy will have to be removed." "A Russian state from the Urals to the North Sea can be no improvement over a German state from the North Sea to the Urals." "A modern, vitalized, and militarized China of 450 million people is going to be a threat not only to Japan, but also to the position of the Western powers in the Asiatic Mediterranean."

There is more concentrated international poison for dealing with the future of the world in the last fifteen pages of his book than in the whole of *Mein Kampf*. Is Professor Spykman raging mad? No, he is talking science, a science that has nothing to do with human values or human beings. He is completely objective, thoroughly detached, hermetically sealed, and sterilized of all normal human sentiments. If anyone can see

---

[29] *Ibid.,* pp. 460-461. See the exact quotation already given in the section "The Emergence of Asia," (pp. 20-21).

any difference in *Weltanschauung* between Spykman and Haushofer or Hitler, I should like to be told. Professor Spykman is intellectually a Nazi, but of course scientific labels carry no stigma in scientific circles. The distinction between a skunk and a squirrel is pure uneducated prejudice. Unless we can come up to this austere intellectual plane of natural science, we cannot understand Professor Spykman.

The American public woke up last year to the realization of the presence of a new word, "geopolitics," or *Geopolitik,* as the Germans say. Connected with it is the name of Major-General Professor Doktor Karl Haushofer (born 1869), its great apostle, who is credited with having exerted a profound influence over Hitler, almost as Rasputin was pictured as an influence on the last of the Russian Czars. Anyway, Chapter XIV of Vol. II of *Mein Kampf* is thought to be pure or adulterated Haushofer. His position in relation to World War II seems to be like that of Treitschke in relation to World War I.

The public belatedly rubs its eyes and then finds that there was an Englishman before Haushofer, Sir Halford MacKinder, who, as far back as 1904, enunciated the central dynamic geopolitical concept of the Euro-asiatic "Heartland," and whose book, *Democratic Ideals and Reality,* published in 1918 and completely forgotten, was recently resuscitated in a 1942 reissue. Then we discover further that the whole biological and dehumanized concept of a "state organism" with "organic lusts," growing and expanding like a plant in its struggle for "living space," was already given its sharp contours by a Swedish professor, Rudolf Kjellén (died 1922), who had learned it from his German master, Friedrich Ratzel (1844-1904), in the eighteen-nineties. The importance of the international origin of this peculiarly European science will be explained later.

What gives geopolitics its dangerous character is, however, the fact that it is called "science," in whose name many crimes have been committed. It must be remembered that the very thing that distinguishes German geopolitics from political ge-

THE SCIENCE OF THE BLOODY EARTH 151

ography is that geopolitics is "a guide to political action." Political geography is primarily geography, whose functions are descriptive and analytical, while geopolitics is primarily politics, the politics of world conquest or at least of world struggles, consciously built on strategic concepts of geography. As the German geopolitician Otto Maull well puts it:

> *Geopolitik* concerns itself with the state, not as a static concept, but as a living being. It is not interested like its mother science, political geography, in the state as a phenomenon of nature—in its situation, size, form, or boundaries as such. Geopolitics . . . is a discipline that weighs and evaluates a given situation and by its conclusions seeks to guide practical politics.[30]

It has therefore the definite character of an applied science. Since the only professed application of this science is the struggle of states for living space through wars for the control of the globe, geopolitics is not the innocuous political science of relations of state organisms to the "soil," but necessarily the science of blood and soil combined. Not that the geopoliticians themselves ever cared a twopence about human blood. That lies outside the "precincts" of this "exact science." But when they talk about the "earth" or the "World Island," I see it dyed pinkish-purple with human blood. It is not the science of the "soil," of land-mass and "Heartland" and "Rimland" and living space and expanding space, but the Science of the Bloody Earth, as different from political geography as slush is different from snow. Its only scientific aspects are its accumulation of factual data, its strictly biological conception of "political space organism" (the state) as a tree growing on the soil or dying for lack of it, and, last of all, that godlike indifference to, and godless contempt for, moral judgments and values which we call complete scientific "objectivity." Populations may be trans-

---

[30] Andreas Dorpalen, *The World of General Haushofer*, pp. 24-25.

planted like carrots, and the "World Island" may be cut up, examined, and redisposed to the advantage of the expanding state like a melon. Whether a few dozen schoolchildren have to be bombed or a million inhabitants slaughtered in the process is unworthy of the concern of such globe-cutters. It is exactly that detachment from human values, that mechanistic concept of physical forces determining human events, and that "naturalistic" view of the human world as a jungle which give it its scientific character.

It is particularly unfortunate that not only does geopolitics arrogate to itself the attitude and terminology of a natural science, but that it is known as German science. I cannot say that the Americans have exactly an inferiority complex with regard to German science. American cameras are probably as good as German cameras, and the American bomb sight is just a damn sight better than the German bomb sight. Nevertheless, German science has always enjoyed a high prestige, for which American academic circles show great respect. German influence in American universities in certain branches of study, as, for instance, in the teaching of literature, is to be deplored and still weighs heavily on our postgraduate schools. The fact that geopolitics goes under the name of German science immediately commands the respect of certain American professors and soon finds it a host of camp followers.

Life reported at the end of 1942: "This year some 1500 courses in geopolitics are being given in United States colleges. On campuses all over the country musty old geographers are blossoming out as shiny new geopoliticians." But there are also first-class minds among American geopoliticians, like President Isaiah Bowman, of Johns Hopkins University, Father Walsh, of Georgetown, Nicholas Spykman, of Yale, Derwent Whittlesey, of Harvard, Edward Mead Earle and Harold Sprout, of Princeton. "Science" it is called, and science it will be. How American common sense will modify Haushoferism remains to be seen, but there is no thought on the part of American professors of disclaiming the scientific title, and we cannot laugh it off as a German poison which will be automatically neutralized as soon as it reaches American soil.

How deeply influenced by this German *Weltanschauung* and by Darwinian naturalism American geopoliticians are, is best seen in Professor Spykman, in whose book this German austerity of the "natural science of power politics" with no room for human values finds a complete, unmitigated reflection. How does a quotation like the following strike the reader?

> The statesman who conducts foreign policy can concern himself with the values of justice, fairness and tolerance only to the extent that they contribute to or do not interfere with the power objective. They can be used instrumentally as moral justification for the power quest, but they must be discarded the moment their application brings weakness. The search for power is not made for the achievement of moral values; moral values are used to facilitate the attainment of power.

Nine out of ten readers would think that this was from *Mein Kampf;* but, no, this is from Spykman's *America's Strategy in World Politics,* page 18. This is the book of which an American university president, Isaiah Bowman, of Johns Hopkins, says, "It should be read in not less than a million American homes. Every government official responsible for policy should read it once a year for the next twenty years."

This moral prostitution of the academic point of view may be further seen in the fact that when Dr. Hans W. Weigert wrote a heartrending appeal for restoration of human values in the last chapter of his new book on geopolitics, *Generals and Geographers,* a reviewer in the *New York Times* said, "The last fifteen pages of the book on 'Geopolitics and Humanity' should never have been written." He declared that the book "concludes with an outlook . . . which is as cloudy and con-

fused as anything Haushofer has ever written." What makes
it "cloudy and confused" to the reviewer, I assume, is the introduction of human values of right and wrong into the austere
plane of objective science. I shudder to think that American
academic reaction to Dr. Weigert's appeal is dead.

On the other hand, the recent books on the subject by
Strausz-Hupé, Derwent Whittlesey, and Andreas Dorpalen,[31]
as well as the one by Hans W. Weigert, have been sanely
critical of Haushoferism. German geopolitical thought deserves to be studied carefully, even as *Mein Kampf* deserves to
be studied carefully. (Dorpalen's *The World of General Haushofer* gives the original source material rarely accessible to the
American public.)

To me, however, geopolitics, Haushoferian or otherwise, is
50 per cent factual data, 30 per cent pseudo-science, and 20 per
cent German metaphysics or "Faustian longing." Since far too
many definitions are being offered, some made purposely innocuous with an air of scientific objectivity, one should accept
Haushofer's own: "Geopolitics is the scientific foundation of
the art of political action in the life-and-death struggle of state
organisms for *Lebensraum*." [32] Take away from it the naturalistic warring concepts of "life-and-death struggle" and "state
organism" and *"Lebensraum"* and it no longer serves any purpose as a guide to political action. Take away from it the dynamic concept of the Eurasian transcontinental bloc based on
the Asiatic Heartland, and it is worth less than a penny to
Haushofer or Hitler himself.

Obviously geopolitics has its contributions. The first is the
notion that political planning of the world for war or for peace
must be based on sound knowledge of geography, just as war

---

[31] Robert Strausz-Hupé, *Geopolitics: the Struggle for Space and Power* (Putnam);
Derwent Whittlesey, *German Strategy of World Conquest* (Farrar and Rinehart),
with interesting illustrations of geopolitical maps; Andreas Dorpalen, *The World of
General Haushofer* (Farrar and Rinehart).

[32] Quoted by Dr. Hans W. Weigert, *Generals and Geographers* (Oxford) p. 14.
See also the many "official" and unofficial definitions in Dorpalen's book, pp. 23-25.

plans require good maps. Vice-President Wallace's proposal for air highways, taking account of the arctic regions, is an excellent geopolitical concept. In a true sense anybody who ever reflected upon the political significance of the Panama Canal or the Suez Canal was thinking geopolitically. The second is that it teaches a global concept of the war and the peace as nothing else can, a concept in which the Germans and the Japanese excel and in which the western democracies are woefully left behind. The best argument for Nazi "war guilt," if one is needed, is the evidence of their preparedness and the dismal political confusion of the democracies with regard to Asia a year after Pearl Harbor. The Germans and the Japanese were excellently prepared in global political strategy, while Anglo-Americans were and are still muddled about Asia. Incidentally, there is also great profit to be derived from the art of drawing dynamic maps and reading them, which can be learned from geopolitics. Haushofer's great complaint when he started the Munich institute was that the German generals did not know how to read maps.

We are pretty well agreed that Rosenberg's racial myth of Aryan superiority is pseudo-science. The question comes closer to the human heart. We do not even bother to disprove it, because our heart denies it. That geopolitics is a pseudo-science is less obvious, because the geopoliticians are apparently talking of land-mass and the contours of the "World Island." That it is nevertheless a pseudo-science arises from the fact that it deals with world politics, and by its very nature world politics cannot be treated with the cold objectivity of, say, mineralogy. There is simply no objectivity possible in dealing with human values. Somewhere a human choice has to be made, and when that choice is made, subjective elements come in. Then geopolitics is as little objective as the Aryan race myth. The hopeless confusion of moral values and the undependableness of such opinions immediately become apparent.

A curious example of this is Professor George T. Renner's

proposal to exterminate the Swiss Republic on geopolitical grounds. The proposal is not only unjust; it is untrue to a human fact, because the Swiss Republic has demonstrated its ability to hang together as a human community living in peace for seven hundred years by certain democratic values beyond the ken of Professor Renner, and in flagrant defiance of the geopolitical "law of expanding space." In the same way, Professor Spykman is geographically fascinated by the similarity of Japan's and England's positions on the map and therefore advocates co-operating with Japan on the same terms as with England, disregarding the human fact that English mentality is not essentially warlike, while Japanese mentality is. Such confusions and contradictions are inevitable. What I object to is that such romantic nonsense, such lack of grasp of world political realities, should seek refuge under the name of science. To contradict common sense does not necessarily indicate a scientific mind.

That geopolitics is a pseudo-science is less easily recognizable because the roots are deeper and fall in line with nineteenth-century naturalism, which is the transferring of the Darwinian concept of life-and-death struggle to the humanities. This naturalism was a characteristic of European thought in the latter part of the nineteenth century. I have referred to the international European character of the origins of geopolitics. It started with Ratzel's conception of "state organism" as a struggling, living thing, and Kjellén's *The State as Living Form*. Unmistakably drawing its inspiration from the Darwinian interpretation of the animal world, the naturalistic tendency was to transpose the laws of the animal world to the human world in the name of science. In his essay "Living-space: A Bio-Geographical Study" (1901), Ratzel clearly used Darwinian terms of the animal world and made no bones about it.

The danger lies in the fact that unless one denied the freedom of the human will and talked of physical forces and mechanical "laws of expanding space" and "organisms," with the nature of topography as a god determining the growth and death of nations, one could not appear "scientific" at all. Furthermore, science wants to predict, and only determinism enables us to predict. In the realm of geopolitical thought Oswald Spengler, whom Haushofer quoted implicitly, expressed most clearly the view of human culture in terms of plant morphology as something rooted in the "soil" and growing and dying with it. His pessimism is a direct result of his determinism, which is again a result of his naturalism. It is because its roots are deep in European thought and in European power politics that we cannot think of Haushofer's development as a local German aberration.

We cannot therefore say that geopolitics has no values; it has a clear set of naturalistic values, the values of power politics or of the law of the jungle. If we accept naturalistic values, we must end up in Spenglerian pessimism; from it there is no escape. Unless we are willing to make a clean break with power politics and with this naturalistic *Weltanschauung,* Spengler's pessimism is justified. Perhaps the western civilization will go down in eternal wars.

The trouble with naturalism is that too many things are becoming natural. The law of the jungle has become natural to our academic minds. Manslaughter has become scientifically natural. The bombing of schoolchildren has become natural also. We have had enough of naturalism. To be inhumanly scientific has ceased to be a reproach with us.

Somewhere we must stop, before we come to the brink of the catastrophe. Unless we are willing to take many things on faith and abjure the false cloak of science, this era of human civilization is doomed. Unless we renounce the intellectual code which has led us to 1914 and to 1939, and render unto natural science what belongs to science and render unto man what belongs to man, I do not see how the western civilization can escape destruction. There are too many things we cannot be scientific about because we can never "prove" them or even measure them. The equality of men and peoples can never be proved. The possibility of world co-operation can never be proved. These things have to be taken on faith. In place of naturalistic values, we have to set up human values. Our very standard and notion of truth itself must be changed. The standard of Confucius is still not far wrong. "Truth must not depart from human nature. If what is regarded as truth departs from human nature, it may not be regarded as truth." That is the Confucian answer to naturalism.

Geopoliticians call themselves "realists," by which they mean they have no patience with ideals. Many of our intellectuals belong to a cynic generation, while the Munich men and other appeasers are regarded as "realists." Those who speak for the freedom of India are laughed at. Those who plead for a complete break with power politics are laughed at. Those who choose to believe that sincere co-operation and good will between the western democracies and Russia are possible by an act of human will, if we will make the effort, are laughed at. Those who are telling the world to go down the bloody path of national suspicions and balance of power call themselves "realists."

At bottom it is only a question of the freedom of the human will versus determinism, the question whether good will has the power to change the world we make for ourselves. Peace on earth, I repeat, is an act of faith, and without faith we shall not be saved. It boils down almost to this: Jesus, the Prince of Peace, was a liar or He was not. We've got to make up our minds.

*

18

THE INTELLECTUAL'S DILEMMA

IT SEEMS that we are the inheritors of a sick and dying tradition in modern thought, from which these professors of geopolitics are not able to lift themselves. In geopolitics and its professed disciples, we see a deep-seated cynicism, a stupid belief in force and necessary struggle, a total absence of appreciation of a moral point of view, and above all, a haughty threat of force in the form of an overwhelming air and sea power with which the world is going to be policed for the world's own good.

If the voice of the professors prevails over the voice of the common people—and there is every evidence that it prevails strongly in certain influential and official sections of the western democracies—the blood of millions of American boys will have to be shed in a future war. For even they themselves do not tell you that, following the pattern of world domination, there will be a world peace, but only that the Anglo-American sword will be ground so sharp and suspended so ominously low over the rest of the world that no revolt will be possible. In other words, while force cannot succeed in Hitler's hands, it can succeed in Anglo-American hands. If this is the sum of wisdom that guides men's actions in politics, then the picture is dark indeed. It simply means the assumption that after the war, the world must be frightened by 50,000 Anglo-American planes and 200,000 pilots. But suppose China refuses to be frightened, Russia refuses to be frightened, and the world refuses to be frightened. Then what? Go out and bomb them after the war? What childish simplicity!

How many millions of American boys must shed their blood in order to crush both China and Russia never concerns the learned professor. If it did, he would cease to be a scientist and would make a disgraceful display of such human emotions as the sense of right and wrong and the revulsion against killing fellow men. Professor Spykman has forgotten about God. His reply is that his subject is strictly geopolitics, and God and geopolitics are separate. My reply to that is that they should not be separate, or we would be debasing the human intellect in the name of science. I know I am a heathen and Professor Spykman is a Christian, but still a heathen can believe in God, and I like to argue with the Christian professor on this point.

The dilemma exists everywhere and must be faced quickly. The academic dilemma in modern scholarship, that in order to be "scientific" we must reject moral judgments and cannot even properly handle human sentiments—in other words, the enforced amorality of the academic point of view—had better be quickly solved by western thinkers, or we must have as a natural result international amorality in human relations. The elimination of conscience has come from the top, not from below, from the educated, not from the uneducated. Consequently, if we are to continue to live safely together, we must rely upon the judgment of the New York taxi-drivers, and not on that of a Yale Professor of International Relations.

For we are getting closer to the deep-seated sores of a curious modern intellectual malady. I accuse western scholarship of being amoral, which is a splendid attitude in the natural sciences, but downright decadent and obscene in the sphere of human studies. I maintain that the academic attitude, deprived of warm emotions for our fellow men, is a dangerous attitude to teach in our college classrooms. I maintain that this trend of thought has produced a Hitler, and will produce more Hitlers wherever this type of moral prostitution prevails. I maintain, further, that this method of strict objectivity, useful in the natural sciences, is unreliable and dangerous in the human sciences. I maintain that objective thinking in human relations is an impossibility and never exists. Consequently, I maintain that no human science, in the sense of a true natural science, is possible, except physiology—and its related studies, medicine and anthropology. I believe that the scientific technique is inadequate in the so-called human sciences and must be supplemented by insight and simple wisdom, and that, unless we do so, we are heading for disaster. Particularly is this true of world problems. In a later chapter, I shall try to make this clear.

I maintain this because, first of all, in the final weighing of conclusions, after the assemblage of facts, the decision is always a subjective process, involving evaluation of imponderable factors, never reducible to facts and figures. An example of the failure of the objective method is the isolationist position of Charles A. Beard. In the final weighing of divergent facts, to arrive at an isolationist or an anti-Axis stand, the emotions not only do, but also *should* enter into our considerations, or we are debasing the intellect and the conscience God has given us.

Secondly, in the realm of human affairs, psychological facts and factors could never be assessed with anything like the accuracy found in the scientific measurement of electric volts or radio waves. Outstanding cases are Russian and Chinese morale. If anybody took the trouble to assemble facts, the Germans certainly did. So did the Japanese. The odds looked all in their favor; the odds do not look that way now. If the Germans could be wrong, so could we.

Thirdly, we all place different values upon human facts, making objectivity impossible. The fact that the Japanese are a warlike nation and the English are a peace-loving nation has a certain significance for me, but not for Professor Spykman. The fact that the Japanese are warlike and aggressive while the Chinese are peace-loving and essentially democratic in their way of life should be the deciding factors in choosing our partners for the postwar world; but it does not seem so to Professor Spykman, who only looks at the map spread out before him and is intellectually intrigued by the similarities in geographical position between England and Japan. Who is really objective, and who can say that he alone is correct—and wise?

Fourthly, he fools only himself who thinks he is free from prejudice. Emotional bias inevitably steps in. Professor Spykman notes that China's position in regard to the Asiatic Mediterranean (Malaysia, etc.) is similar to that of the United States in regard to the American Mediterranean (the Caribbean Sea). Nevertheless, he thinks of the necessity of creating a strong Japan to check China, while he would never for a moment think of creating a strong Mexico to check the United States. That final decision is pure emotional prejudice.

Fifthly, back of all such fascist thought is the fashionable determinism of modern scholarship. Determinism always spells irresponsibility, as if we were by necessity helpless to create a better world to live in. The taxi-driver has the courage to say, "This world of eternal wars is bad; let's change it." The determinist has not the courage to say so, but must say, "It is bad, and will continue to be bad." There is a curious intellectual delight in such satanic predictions, but it is not going to help build a better world. The elimination of conscience from western scholarship has gone far enough.

Sixthly, the world is not so simple as these pseudo-scientists like to imagine. What the unpredictable effects of Anglo-American domination by an overwhelming force will be, the best geopoliticians cannot tell us. Only one thing we know definitely: the greatest force produces the greatest hatred. The normal human reaction against all threats of force, the corruption that will set in with power, and the guilty conscience that follows corruption, the dilemma of sending American boys to help England fight a native insurrection in New Delhi or Calcutta, the absolute certainty of the willingness of Russians, Chinese, and Indians to be bombed to pieces and continue sullen resistance, the meeting of violence with nonviolence, which should burn Christian cheeks but doesn't, the groaning under the crushing burdens of taxation for armaments, and the final wise and happy intuition of the Kansas farmer, "Damn it all, why should I police the world for others!"—all such things are bound to follow in its wake, resulting in a violent reaction such as followed the Versailles Treaty.

The advocates of such sheer domination by force have not even the wit to see these things. In any case, the guilt of arming against Russia and China will lie heavily upon the American conscience, and moral defeatism will set in long before an actual war between the races sets off the final and greatest conflagration of the world.

IV. DIAGNOSIS

19

THE CHARACTER OF THE MODERN AGE

WHY all this disillusionment? Evidently man's way of thinking has changed. The meaning and value of life have changed. Man's conception of himself has changed. Our idea of the nature of man has changed, and when that changes, the world itself goes through an upheaval. Let us make this historically clear.

A world tragedy seems a convenient time and compelling ground for assessing the character of an age and taking count of appreciations and depreciations of our spiritual stocks. Our complacency about European civilization is gone. Every time I think of Europe, I think of a photograph of three Poles hanged by the Germans, the ropes around their necks suspended from a common rack, their bodily frames unduly stretched and gaunt and long. It doesn't matter to me whether the Germans are hanging Poles, or the Poles are hanging Germans: what this means to me is simply this, that Europeans are hanging Europeans. That photograph is a comment, a profound comment, on modern European civilization.

When you survey the march of the last four centuries since the coming of the Modern Age, you are dismayed at the appreciation and depreciation of certain intellectual currencies, called "ideas." Do not forget the social and economic unrest in Europe that preceded this war—the disintegration and collapse of democratic values, the search for sheer security, the security in mere making of a living, which caused the rise of Fascism, Nazism, Socialism, Communism, and all forms of collectivism. Against this background picture, let us take the following inventory, with "dep.," "app.," "s.q.a.," "w.o.," and "sl." standing for *depreciation, appreciation, status quo ante, wiped out,* and *slight* respectively:

	God	Soul	Free-dom	Educa-tion	Indus-trial Wealth	Social Wel-fare	Human Rights	Eco-nomic Rights
U. S. S. R.	dep.	s.q.a.	dep.	app.	app.	app.	dep.	app.
Germany	w.o.	s.q.a.	w.o.	app.	app.	app.	w.o.	s.q.a.
France	dep.	dep.	dep.	app.	app.	?	dep.	?
England	sl.dep.	sl.dep.	s.q.a.	app.	app.	app.	s.q.a.	app.

On the whole, God and freedom fare the worst and education and industrial wealth fare the best. It is interesting to note that the notion of the soul (*Seele*) has not at all depreciated in modern Germany, but is a driving force in the German war machine. "Freedom" is contrasted with regimentation, and stands for the rights of the individual, or the "Human Rights," which column is therefore redundant except as a convenient visual contrast with the "Economic Rights." We are talking more and more about the right to a job, right to an income, right to security against unemployment and old age, the rights covered by the Beveridge Plan, the right of the soldier to come back and find work, etc., and are talking less and less about the right to be free, the right of national sovereignty, and the right of the individual. "Industrial Wealth" stands for the nation's industrial productivity and does not refer to the distribution of wealth. Volume of wealth in itself without relation to its distribution means nothing to the individual and cannot indicate progress, but is only a measure of war potential to the nation. In fact, industrial overproductivity starts the race for markets and must end in the war for markets; it is highly questionable whether it is a factor contributing toward peace rather than the reverse. Industrial nations start wars, agricultural nations don't—witness Japan and China. It has no relation to social peace or unrest, but rather tends, when its products are unevenly distributed, toward unrest. Confucius says, "I have heard that the heads of states and families do not worry about the shortage of people, but worry about inequality of distribution. They do not worry about poverty, but about social unrest. For with equal distribution, there is no poverty, with social unity, there is no shortage of people, and with social peace, there is no danger of collapse." The old man sometimes does hit the nail on the head even in economics!

The off-hand table above is not entirely representative of the progress of Europe, for many of the most socially advanced countries, like Denmark and Holland, are not represented. In Catholic countries God tends to keep his ground; I am not a Catholic, but one has to admit it. But on the whole it is an unhealthy picture, an unsound balance sheet. God and freedom are losing ground. That is why the people of Germany and Italy put up with the suppression of liberty under Fascism, and the very liberals in America are better advocates of economic security than disciples of eighteenth-century freedom.

What does this mean? Man's minds naturally concentrate on the more pressing problems of the age. A man who has an ulcered stomach thinks and talks about nothing but his stomach; I never give mine a thought. The problems of the nineteenth century happened to be economic. The nineteenth century, therefore, talked of economics, as the eighteenth century talked of Reason, and the seventeenth century talked of Divine Purpose. The twentieth century is now talking only of security. Isn't this ominous?

Economic security, by all means; the Beveridge Plan, by all means. Economic unrest is threatening the collapse of capitalist society and, I take it, the Allies are fighting to preserve capitalist society. The war started with social and economic unrest and the collapse of democracy in Europe; when the war is over, naturally we shall pick up from there, and have to plan for it now—that is "postwar planning," which is occupied with full employment, social insurance, etc. These ideas fill our thoughts to the exclusion of everything else. From domestic economics, we go on to international economics, and we confuse international peace with a satisfactory international balance sheet. The school of Cordell Hull seems to think that the maintenance of world peace is merely a matter of readjusting the tariff tables, and that good will, justice, liberty, and human brotherhood simply flow from a prosperous international business year.

In my recent years of stay in the United States, I have met only one thinking American, at least the only one thinking about peace whose values agree with mine. That man is a Negro. Several months ago I was talking with a Negro porter at the Union Station in Washington. His face was very intelligent and very sad. I learned he had finished three years of high school in the Middle West. He was making about $150 a month, with which he had to keep a family with four children. I started talking with him because there was something deep in his eyes. I said he was doing well in wartime, but he said it was hard and his wife and the eldest daughter had to go out to work. Then we started talking about the war. Sadly he remarked, "Conditions may change—perhaps—after the war. But it isn't the money I'm complaining about. I don't mind working for little money. It is that we want to be treated and thought of as human beings." His words, spoken simply and sincerely, stung me. Are you going to give him relief by some American Beveridge Plan? But a point like that is what we cannot solve by mathematics and what the western thinkers are entirely unaware of in their postwar planning. They are thinking very hard about his economic rights, and not thinking at all about his human rights. They assume he will be happy with his economic rights.

On the other hand, we are told to give up more and more freedom; that arouses the true democrat's blood. The economic remedy is for curing certain economic ills, it is not a cure-all. The cure for the ills of economic progress is not more economic progress. Man has still to go on and so live that he finds life both good and enjoyable. What if we win the war and lose the soul? Civilization after all must have a content.

Yet the matter goes deeper than that. It reaches down to the roots and fiber of our thinking and has something to do with the temper of the age. And I make the categorical statement: *With our way of thinking, we cannot create or devise a world peace.* Modern thinking is increasingly mechanical. May I point out how the very phraseology of the modern tongue has changed? We are today scared of the old simple words, like "goodness," "justice," and "mercy." These are still possible to use, but, for instance, a phrase like "human brotherhood" would at once condemn its user to the charge of empty rhetoric and unclear thinking. It is something this age simply doesn't believe in, at least in the highbrow circles. Contrast it with the French word *"Fraternité";* once upon a time, it was capable of arousing intense emotions even among the intellectuals. They just believed in it; we moderns just don't. This age shuns moral platitudes, and *goodness, justice,* and *mercy* seem like overused coins. We create euphemisms for these words and would rather speak of them as anything but goodness, justice, and mercy. A girl with a Victorian name like "Faith," "Prudence" or "Patience" would be the laughingstock of her schoolmates. Educators, preachers, and publicists generally evade these words by using a more modern term; they call them the "spiritual values" or the "social values." But this particular use of the word "value" is strange, for it derives from economics. It has some relation to the ledger and therefore has a good, old, reassuring tone, reminding one of the "good values" that a housewife admires on a bargain counter. Other words derive from the social sciences. Educators speak of prostitutes and prostitution as "anti-social beings" and "anti-social behavior." Such phrases have a queer, dehydrated, synthetic flavor and suggest that the bones of our morality have been picked pretty clean. We don't reform a drunkard any more, we just "readjust" him to society as we readjust a watch, or even possibly "acclimatize" him to a new environment. A successful or unsuccessful man is an "integrated" or "divided" or "maladjusted" personality. The words of the modern tongue are getting increasingly mechanical. Both a political party and a motor-car are a "machine." Public sentiments are "response" or "reactions," diplomatic communications are "pressure," and a popular attitude is just "habitual mass-conditioning." Pride is "inflated ego," bravado is a "defense mechanism," criticism is an "outlet," and something or other is a "safety valve," and somebody out of a job is just a "dislocated" individual.

I am choosing very general terms that have nothing to do with a personal style, and I exclude such specific academic jargon of sociologists and psychologists as "processes of equalization of satisfaction value," "emotive reaction," "ideational reorientation," and "associative memory response." The plain fact is, we are scared not only of moral judgments, but of all normal emotions. Our morality is getting a little synthetic and is served up to the public in dehydrated essences. But if anybody tells me that psychologists who talk of "associative memory response" can educate good human beings or sociologists who talk of "equalization of satisfaction value" can help the society of man, I simply refuse to believe him. In an interesting article on this type of "pedagese" in *The American Scholar* (Winter, 1942-1943), the writer quotes such interesting curiosities from teachers who are supposed to teach our young and to communicate some kind of enthusiasm for learning. "The Reduction of Data Showing Non-Linear Regression for Correlation by the Ordinary Product-Moment Formula; and the Measurement of Error Due to Curvilinear Regression" was the title of a paper read before the Psychology Section of the American Association for the Advancement of Learning! The development of a child's interest in history or geography or wit or wisdom is to be discovered by "an extension of the Kelley-Wood and the Kondo-Elderton Tables of Abscissae of the Unit Normal Curve, for Arcas ($\frac{1}{2}$a) between .4500 and .49999 99999." When I see such teachers, shall I not say like Jesus, "Suffer the little children to come unto me"? The machine has been substituted for the man, and one could feel from the use of these mechanical terms that the human mind itself is being changed and that a kind of scientific formalin is taking the place of human blood in our blood vessels. Through the Funeral Directory of Science we must go and have our blood replaced by formalin before we can come out as university professors and teachers of this age. The human mind itself is a "track," single or double. God Himself is a sort of Center of Gravity. Only the dollar is still a dollar, unless it is fifty-nine cents.

And so, before we can understand ourselves and this age, we must understand the roots of our present thinking, and see how we came to think in this curious twentieth-century way at all. Why have the standards changed? Why has our conception of man changed? Why has the meaning of life gone? Why, in particular, do we come to be the cynics, pessimists, and hard-boiled "realists" that we are even in the midst of a war for democracy? Materialists must fight to the end of eternity. Materialists cannot end war or create peace. *They have not the brains for it.* Why, then, are we materialists?

Let us take the idea of Freedom, and see how its basis is failing. We shall see how the very content of Freedom has changed, because the idea of man's "rights," on which Freedom is based, has changed.

But first I must make clear that two of the Four Freedoms are not freedoms at all, and one of them has no meaning for me. A study of the Four Freedoms reveals that there are two "doubles" masquerading as Freedom that the Devil Economics has put there. Freedom from fear is not freedom, but political security. Freedom from want is not freedom, but economic security. Both may be achieved at the cost of human freedom, and probably will, if we think too much about animal security. Nothing gives such a feeling of perfect freedom from want and fear to a dog as a collar around its neck. Its next meal is guaranteed. A bird in a cage has exchanged its freedom on the wing for freedom from the preying hawk and freedom from starvation in the snow. But a bird which deliberately flies into a cage cannot be said to be fighting for its freedom except by the most caustic casuistry. It is a mere trick of the English language, and "freedom *from* want" or "fear" is untranslatable into Chinese or French. What is *"liberté de misère"* or *"liberté de peur"?* We may, if we like, easily add a few more freedoms, like "Freedom from Disease," which is health, and "Freedom from Dirt," which is cleanliness, and "Freedom from the Telephone," which is peace and rest, *ad infinitum.* The Indians might add "Freedom from England," which is genuine human and political freedom. And so when we speak of freedom, we must stick to the original meaning of the term, without "of" and without "from"— just plain good old freedom—human freedom. It is possible for man to have all the Four Freedoms—the freedom to talk and think as he pleases and to be fed and sheltered in security —and yet be a slave.

The freedom of belief has a peculiarly American and seventeenth-century context, for the people of the Thirteen Colonies were pilgrims or religious refugees, who came to America that they might worship the God they chose and in the way they chose. But freedom of belief does not have such a ring in Chinese ears; it has absolutely no meaning to a Chinese, and it is not what the Chinese are fighting for. In the absence of religious wars and persecutions, freedom of belief is just accepted in Chinese national life; to fight for it is like taking an oath to fight for and maintain the blueness of the sky. Freedom of speech has been interfered with in certain periods of Chinese history, as in western democracies, and therefore it has still some meaning. But it is not broad enough, and is distinctly less comprehensive than just human freedom. I would not go to war with anybody just to protect freedom of speech; I could do with silence, or get around it to say all I want to say without landing in jail. I would consider as a worthy objective of this war only good old freedom, the freedom of all races and all peoples on this earth. On this issue we may not evade. Nor may we be less explicit about the freedom of the individual.

Nevertheless, the word "Freedom" has still a beautiful ring in America and the world. It means that the common people still believe in it—in plain old, human freedom. It is a slightly overused coin, but it is still a good penny. You can still set not only Americans, but Hindus, Chinese, Greeks, Negroes, and Finns fighting for it, with the blood surging in their veins. And that is what the majority of the peoples of the world are fighting for. To me it is a sort of come-down and sounds a little comical, as it must sound to the humorous American soldier, to say "Kill the Japs! Kill the Germans! So that you may come back and only work 40 hours a week at $75.00, with medical insurance and time and a half for overtime!" My blood reaction would not register. Something must be wrong with the economic view of man.

But how did the idea of "freedom" arise? How did the Rights of Man arise? How did that word happen to have that fine, revolutionary ring to it? It was created as an answer to oppression and a call to rebellion. When circumstances of political oppression exist, the word "freedom" always recovers that rousing, revolutionary ring. When Patrick Henry shouted, "Give me liberty or give me death," it reached depths in the hearts of the American people, because the oppression was there. When Jawaharlal Nehru shouts, "Give me liberty or give me death," it leaves the Bertrand Russells and Norman Angells cold because they don't happen to be the oppressed. Even to the Americans, it is something so remote that it is less important than diplomatic etiquette; silence is preferable to breaking the punctilio between the august governments. To intervene on the principle of a nation's freedom would be almost as bad as putting the wife of the British Ambassador below the wife of the Brazilian Minister at a Washington diplomatic dinner. It would be almost uncivilized. Dr. Wellington Koo is said to have intervened on behalf of the Chinese Government for India before his departure. But it was such a hideous *faux pas* that Winston Churchill is reported to have told him that if the Chinese Government did not stop intervening in the matter, British-Chinese relations would be seriously endangered! That is how far the word "freedom" has fallen in the thinking of man in the twentieth century!

In the eighteenth century freedom came in with the human "rights." Now it happens both "human rights" and the modern "economic rights" are myths, from a philosophical standpoint. They were, and are, simply things that men strongly believed or believe in. Like God and the soul, these "rights" could never be proved. If we want them badly enough, we say God gave them to us. Like the Divine Right of Kings, they were categorical statements. Heine called the Divine Right of Kings "the twaddle of tonsured quacks." And so the Rights of Man had also a theological basis. Thomas Jefferson held these truths to be "self-evident." Moreover, we were "created equal" and "born free" and these rights were "unalienable," so that metaphysically neither King nor God could take them away from us. But how did we know that we were "created equal," or "born free"? We simply chose to believe so. But Rousseau's naïve picture of the savage and the natural man has long been exploded by science. That man is "born free" was merely a statement of passionate belief. Like the Divine Right of Kings, it had no rational or scientific basis, and when men were ready to discard them, they simply withdrew the theological structure from underneath. Historically, different nations have spoken of "rights of commerce," "rights to trade" in other countries, and simultaneously the rights to exclude others from trade or labor in their own country; conquering nations speak of "the right to expansion" or to "living space"; a few go further and discover a Divine Destiny to Rule a particular region, and fishing nations speak of the "right to take salmon."

Similarly, when we want the right to a job or employment badly enough, we shall also be speaking of the "divine right to work," or to a salary or pension, or that men are "born employed," and at times it may even look more important to be "born employed" than to be "born free" or "born equal." If we don't look out, someday we may discover that we are "born to a coupon," with the "inalienable right to a coupon" that no one shall metaphysically be able to take away from us. Fundamentally, that is why we are forsaking the human rights and switching over to the economic rights.

So then the spiritual "values" are slipping and leave a vacuum. *Liberté, egalité, fraternité* have lost their prophetic Messianic ring. Equalitarianism seems to have fallen into disrepute. Democratic values, economic values, security values are being thrown into a witches' cauldron from which arises only a steam stinking with a strong totalitarian smell. Into this vacuum rush the confusing ideologies, and Communists, Socialists and Democrats exchange blows in the dark, not knowing who is fighting whom. Stalin is calling the U.S.S.R. a "democracy," and the Archbishop of Canterbury may be properly classified as a "red" by the *N. Y. Journal-American*. As for Pétain, he needs no ideology for his regime at all; it is neither Fascist, nor Socialist, nor Republican; he is neither Fuehrer, nor Duce, nor Dictator, nor President. For his ideology, he merely gasps "Work, Home, and Country!" No, it does not look as if there is going to be peace in Europe. The good old values have gone.

But while we are arguing about the content of freedom and raising the question whether the concept of human freedom has not changed, we are threatened with another more serious and more fundamental matter, which has come about entirely unnoticed, and that is, *Freedom of the Will has disappeared.* Unless we recapture freedom of the will, we shall not have the strength to restore human freedom, and unless we restore human freedom, we shall accomplish nothing with the Four Freedoms, even if we attain them. Why has the Freedom of the Will disappeared?

20

ORIGINS OF THE MECHANISTIC MIND

SUPPOSE we put the matter this way. Power politics is gunpowder politics, and gunpowder politics must end in an explosion. Power politics works with the balance of power, like two supercharged carbons, steadily approaching each other from a distance. As the machines advance, power accumulates, and the final explosions inevitably grow bigger and bigger. We have now reached the stage when explosions of power politics are global in scope. Playing with power politics today is playing with fire. Meanwhile, our moral development lags behind; our thinking is national and not global. The fact must be faced at this moment that *world politics is power politics and it is the only politics we know or can conceivably practice, and that we are in certainty heading for still greater wars and conflicts, however the combinations of power may alter.* And we are accepting this fact with a sense of fatalistic resignation. We have to admit that all our statesmen are power politicians, that both the conduct of the war and the conception of the peace are based on the principle of power politics. We believe that force will continue to rule the world. Professor Spykman is probably right in saying that after the war we shall start where we left off, and world politics will continue to be based on a power pattern. If we accept this thesis, it means that we are heading for greater and greater world struggles until finally one tyrant power dominates all the rest, or European civilization goes down in ruins before that point is reached.

But if you ask, why must we go on with power politics, even though we clearly see the end, the answer is a mechanistic conception of human life—that there is a sort of mechanical inevitability about it, and that we can do nothing about it, much as we would wish to. There is the naturalistic view of the struggle of nations for survival, there is the fundamental materialistic background, and there is the determinism of human affairs which we have unconsciously borrowed from a deterministic view of the physical universe as governed by mechanistic laws. All these viewpoints smack of "science" and give them a certain respectable character. From this point on, power politics assumes not a divine sanction, but a kind of scientific sanction, and political "realism" is identified with clear scientific thinking, while any form of sentimental idealism is suspect of being "moronic." This mechanistic conception of human life naturally ends in despair: after all, human society is a jungle fight for survival. It is almost as if one would say, "We would rather walk with our eyes open to Hell in this

life-and-death struggle of nations for power, than be sentimental idiots that dream about a heaven of peace that nowhere
exists—and may the Devil take the hindmost!"

How did the modern man come to think this way? Psycho-
analytic patients are told to go over their childhood history
and search the hidden corners of their souls for frustrations,
fixations, and complexes, and thus come to understand themselves. Reminiscence brings detachment and understanding
and understanding brings emancipation. A little reminiscing
across the centuries will do the world a lot of good. The modern world will then understand itself. How did we come to
be naturalists, determinists, and materialists?

The dead hand of Science is upon the West. Science or the
objective study of matter has colored man's thinking and
brought us all three, Naturalism, Determinism, and Materialism. Science therefore has destroyed the human values. Naturalism has destroyed the belief in the power for good and
co-operation. Materialism has destroyed subtlety and insight
and faith in things unseen. Determinism has destroyed the
capacity for hope.

I know that the natural scientists will not be offended; in
fact, they will all agree with me and protest the loudest that
their method and their point of view have been stolen and
applied to illegitimate fields, for which they are entirely without
responsibility. The line between natural sciences and the human
studies must be sharply redrawn; the very standards of truth
in both branches of study must be kept distinct. Science deals
with facts, and the human studies deal with values, and neither
need ape the other's technique. Science deals by definition with
exact, classified knowledge, and there is a large realm of important human knowledge that cannot be exact or classified.
If science cannot with its test tubes and chemical agents, produce an answer to such a simple question as "why I like you,"
how can it possibly deal with the question of human relations?

But we have now confused the two groups: human and

natural studies, and a dangerous result follows. The natural scientist says merely, "God, freedom, and the goodness of man are not exact knowledge, and do not lie in my field." But the unnatural scientist, the professor of human studies, says, "God, freedom, and the goodness of man lie within my department, but they cannot be handled scientifically, and if I wish to be a scientist, which certainly I do, I am compelled to ignore them and look somewhere else for mechanical laws. Only in that way can I hope to be modern and keep my job. Furthermore, since science cannot discover God, the soul, and the goodness of man, perhaps they do not exist at all." There the confusion begins. The natural scientist says, "I am only interested in facts." It is the unnatural scientist, compelled to deal with human values but nevertheless feeling bound to ape the scientist's technique, who says, "I am interested in facts also. Neither God, nor freedom, nor the soul is a demonstrable fact. We simply have no means of handling them, and therefore must ignore them, except insofar as they have a body, if any." The natural scientist says, "I measure electric volts and radio waves and plot curves." The unnatural scientist says, "I want to measure and to plot curves also. I want to measure hope, aspirations, ideas, God, and freedom, and I cannot do so. But I can measure populations, birth-rates, food supplies, mechanical response to stimuli, the consonants and vowels of poetry, export and import figures, and the influence of physical environment. In that direction alone lies my hope of being called a scientist."

Since the human studies had to be "sciences," they had to deal with those physical factors of man and of human history which the scientific technique could handle, and it could handle always only the material. The outstanding contributions of the nineteenth and twentieth centuries in the human studies have therefore been along the lines of the influence of physical factors, of climate upon history (Huntington), of occupation upon outlook (Marx), of heredity upon character (Lombroso), of race upon history (Houston Stewart Chamberlain), of environment upon ethics (Westermarck), of eyestrain upon genius (some German doctor), and I shall not be surprised if some historian is able to prove the influence of African beetroots on the Napoleonic war, or if some new prophet is able to demonstrate the influence of nutrition on good morals, or of riboflavin on optimistic thinking. It will be typically modern, and it will sound immensely wise. Many of these are contributions to human thought; some are illuminating, some are laudable, but all of them seem to suffer from a mental squint.

It is easy therefore to understand the direction of intellectual development of the past century, characterized by this technique borrowed from the natural sciences. But along with the change of technique came inevitably a change in *Weltanschauung,* which is a materialistic view of man and of human history and the forces governing our lives. Each little contribution emphasized this aberration slightly, but the total result has turned out to be frightening, as we can see now.

Hence arise the conscientious, diligent fact-finding and fact-verification of Niebuhr and Ranke and the economic interpretation of history of Charles A. Beard, the physiological psychology of Wundt and the behaviorist psychology of J. B. Watson, the "experimental novel" of Zola and the postmortem "realism" of Dreiser and Farrell, the literary criticism of Taine and the research into "origins" of Renan, the "social physics" of Comte and the "materialistic dialectic" of Marx, the "ontological criticism" of poetry of some academic professor and the "comparisons" and "influences" of comparative literature of our postgraduate schools, the incestuous complex of Freud and the looking for the soul (Psyche) in the anus-to-*mons-veneris* area of the psychoanalysts. The whole structure of psychoanalysis falls if there is no seat to our pants. And symbolizing this universal break-up, we have the coterie small talk of T. S. Eliot, the lugubrious self-dissection and exhibitionism of Joyce, and the retreat from harmony of Stravinsky, the retreat from beauty of Picasso, the retreat from logic and sanity of Dali, and the retreat from grammar of Gertrude Stein. In world politics it emerges as the "cultural morphology" of Spengler, the geopolitics of Haushofer, and the economic panacea of Cordell Hull. In the conduct of this war, it becomes the absence of spiritual principles in dealing with Asia and North Africa. Every one of these tendencies smacks of the "scientific." But good taste has vanished, and the meaning of life, apart from assurance of the next meal, has become zero. The only whimper we can hear now is, "Give me security, or give me death! Put me in a collectivistic jail if you want, but give me a meal ticket and an old-age coupon!" What a come-down for a revolutionist! What amazing contrast to the hope of man in the eighteenth century!

For having dealt so successfully with matter, man has become a part of matter. The idea of the nature of man has changed. The force of "ideas" itself has been rejected in history. The study of potsherds has replaced that of the ambitions and loves and hatreds of man in history. Homer is getting better understood, or at least verified, by measurements of broken tiles in ancient Trojan ruins. Historians are more interested in the chamber pots used by Egyptian queens than in their passions and wiles. The search for facts and verification of facts goes on. And a professor of history, holding a precious broken Etruscan jar, exclaims with satisfaction, "We know history."

The search for verifiable facts goes on. While historians measure potsherds, educators measure man's intelligence, criminologists measure human skulls, psychologists measure our impulses and response, geographers measure inches of rainfall, and geopoliticians measure the supply of oil in the Caucasus. If potsherds are understood, history is established; if units of knowledge are properly measured, education is successful; if skulls, jaws, and ears are measured, criminals are as understandable as a washing machine; if impulses and response are properly studied, the whole of man's psyche, his intellect, imagination, will, and ambition and idiosyncrasies are revealed; if rainfall is measured, the rise and decline of civilizations are accounted for; if the control of oil supply is assured, the war is won.

And man has become an atom in a whirling machine, made from the star-dust of some exploded universe. Glands, vessels and liquids make up our bodies, as mechanical inhibitions, conditioned reflexes and complexes make up our minds. Of physical hunger, we know a great deal, of spiritual hunger we know next to nothing. Desires are urges, over which we have as little control as the shape of our skulls. Man is a chemical compound, acted upon by secretions from within and environment from without. The elusive Psyche, unknown, unverifiable, and uncared for, has taken wings and gone. The rainbow has been successfully dissected, the childhood wonder and fancy have gone, and the world has grown gray with us.

Professor Hocking, in one of the most intuitive passages of modern writing, has summarized it well:

It is not strange that with the complete victory, scientific method overshot its mark. Instead of saying, "We have no place for the purposes or values of things in our laboratories," it said in effect, "We have now dismissed purposes and values from the universe." There was a certain satisfaction in a clean sweep: the tedious announcements of the precise purposes of God by pious moralizers could not come back. And so long as science was mainly occupied with the stars and the atoms, this vacuum of value caused no uneasiness.

But the time was to come when science turned its well-trained objective eye on living things and on man. The sciences of psychology and sociology rose like tropical suns, endowed with the initial momentum of an inherited method. Psychology was to be a sort of physics of the passions and thoughts; and man was to be a thing of fact and law. This seemed to be a little hard on freedom, for it inserted the human body exactly and without remainder into the mathematically perfect, and therefore calculable, channels of physical necessity. But, after all, one must yield to the combined force of fact and method; man may quite well retain his feeling of freedom, without actually being free from the laws of nature. So it was assumed.

What was not at first noticed is that *man had become meaningless*. He had become an integral part of the astronomical machine, which had already been renovated and all lurking values thrown into the rubbish heap. The universe was not going anywhere, it was just going! And if the whole show has no purpose, then the human part of it—however it may feel to itself—is again just a fact, a complex and interesting fact, but a transitory fact, together with all its achievements and so-called civilizations. While it is going on, it may glow with subjective light and warmth: but the truth lies with the final sum, and the final sum is a zero of meaning.[33]

It has never been sufficiently pointed out that Hitler's ethics and politics had something to do with this century and a half of European development. Nor has it been pointed out that Hitler's glorification of the irrational (subjection of reason and glorification of the primitive) coincided exactly in time with the glorification of the irrational in Stravinsky, Gertrude Stein, Dali, and Epstein. In fact, it went back to the Romantic revolt against reason, the restoration of the brute will in Nietzsche, and the postmortem picture of the nineteenth century in Max Nordau. Any analysis of the origins of Nazi thought as exclusively Germanic, which excludes the elements of general decay in all western Europe, is self-deceptive. The zero of meaning had been reached: the intellectual atmosphere had been sufficiently purged of classical concepts by a host of scientific researchers; the last glow of Mid-Victorian ethics had gone

---

[33] William Ernest Hocking, *What Man Can Make of Man* (Harper), pp. 31-32.

out; man had in Europe's mind become a mechanistic animal fighting in a fury of blind atoms governed by blind forces. Hitler merely stepped into the vacuum. Otherwise the question "How come Hitler?" can never be answered.

I have written elsewhere:

> It can be proved that the world has gone to pieces as a direct result of scientific materialism invading our literature and thought. The professors of the humanities are reduced to the position of finding mechanistic laws governing human activities, and the more rigorous the "natural laws" can be proved to be, and the more freedom of the will is proved to be a chimera, the greater is the professor's intellectual delight. . . . For scientific materialism must spell determinism and determinism must spell despair. It is therefore no accident that the most admired spirits of our times, not the greatest, but the most in vogue, are pessimists. Our international chaos is founded upon our philosophic despair.[34]

So now when we ask the professor of the humanities, "What are you yourself?" the professor can only reply, brows knitted and head low, "I am a fact also." Where is the call for moral effort, the ringing voice of St. Paul to enter the good race, and the rousing, resounding call of Buddha to achieve the highest of freedoms, the freedom of the spirit? Buddha at least understands the freedom of the will, the power of the human spirit to overcome and transcend the wheel of the material world:

> Rouse thyself by thyself, examine thyself by thyself; thus self-protected and attentive wilt thou live happily, O Bikkshu!
>
> For self is the lord of self, self is the refuge of self; therefore curb thyself as the merchant curbs a noble horse.

---

[34] *The Wisdom of China and India*, p. 574.

By one's self the evil is done, by one's self one suffers; by one's self evil is left undone, by one's self one is purified. The pure and the impure stand and fall by themselves, *no one can purify another.*

You yourself must make an effort. The Tathagatas (Buddhas) are only preachers. The thoughtful who enter the way are freed from the bondage of Mara.[35]

Perhaps we have the freedom of will and of effort. From this belief in the power of the spirit and the human will come the faith and strength and joy of Buddha in man's struggle against the Evil ("Mara") and the bondage of illusion ("Maya").

If anything is to be done, let a man do it, let him attack it vigorously! A careless pilgrim only scatters the dust of passion more widely.

If a man commits a sin, let him not do it again; let him not delight in sin: the accumulation of evil is painful.

If a man does what is good, let him do it again, let him delight in it: the accumulation of good is delightful.

Earnest among the thoughtless, awake among the sleepers, the wise man advances like a racer, leaving behind the hack.

He whose conquests cannot be reconquered, into whose conquest no one in this world enters, by what track can you lead him, the Awakened, the Omniscient, the trackless?

He whom no desire with its snares and poison can lead astray, by what track can you lead him, the Awakened, the Omniscient, the trackless?

Who knows but Buddha may be scientifically more correct than J. B. Watson? Fatalism, in the form of scientific determinism, is perhaps the world's last modern superstition. A

---

[35] *Dhammapada.* See *Wisdom of China and India*, pp. 321-326.

fellow can at least have the courage of his convictions, and stand alone, if necessary.

> If a traveler does not meet with one who is better, or his equal, let him keep to his solitary journey; there is no companionship with a fool.

I, for one, shall not join the international fellowship of fools. Perhaps the world of power politics is only an illusion, in Buddhist terms a "Maya." Perhaps determinism in human affairs is a mirage we create to delude ourselves. Perhaps the prophecy of necessary conflict of power and ruin is such an illusion, and we are merely in the temporary grip of its power, coming barely a century after the fashion for the talk of mechanical laws began. Perhaps we can change the world we make for ourselves. Is this a sermon? No, it is a prayer.

Or, the world shall progress from power to greater agglomeration of powers, from conflict to greater conflicts. The politics of democracy, aristocracy, and monarchy are known; the politics of a world state are not yet even born. The first principles of world democracy, which must be like those of a state democracy, based on the consent of the governed, are not yet established. The world state shall be shaped like a plutocracy, or an oligarchy of the rich, and shall be as insecure as an oligarchy, with a caste of citizens and a caste of slaves. Government shall be based essentially on coercion, and not on consent. There will be rebellion of the masses and bloodshed, and a tyrant shall take the place of the oligarchs, when they are exhausted after fighting the masses and fighting among themselves. For after every revolution and period of chaos appears a tyrant. After the oligarch nations shall have exhausted themselves in a series of wars, a world tyrant, bidding for the support of the masses, shall arise and dominate the world. Is this a prophecy? No, it is a warning.

But some of our leaders have misconstrued the nature of

the world conflict and the present world revolution. The central issue of empire versus world freedom remains unrecognized and unsolved. Some imagine they can fight for empire and freedom at the same time. Winston Churchill is proceeding upon the principles of Pericles. Judged by the principles of the empire, England could have no better and stronger premier. He has the firmness of Lord Clive and Warren Hastings, the singleness of purpose of William Pitt, the astuteness and sense of timing of Disraeli. At a time of national unpreparedness he galvanized the nation with an iron will; in the hour of danger he stood firm; toward rebellions he showed uncompromising strength; when public convictions were failing, he restored impeccable faith in the good old British Empire. But while Disraelis and William Pitts may have been good enough for the Great Britain of the nineteenth and eighteenth centuries, they are not good enough for the modern world. For Churchill has misread the signs of the times. Is this the voice of hostile criticism? No, it is the voice of a friend.

If I do not misinterpret Winston Churchill, he is fighting a twentieth-century war in order to take off his boots after the war and climb back into a nineteenth-century bed, comfortably mattressed in India, Singapore, and Hong Kong. He has the admirable tenacity of the English bulldog, and also its intelligence. Judged by Empire standards, he is a giant; judged by some future and better world, he is no better and no worse than Cato shouting, *"Delenda est Carthago!"* He may even emerge as Scipio the Younger himself, but I seemed to see the Punic Wars being fought all over again, as Rommel and Montgomery struggled in Tunisia for the ancient site of Carthage. To me at present, this seems like the Fourth Punic War. Some Hannibal may invade Italy via Spain with tanks instead of elephants, but the struggle for supremacy over the Mediterranean is neither modern nor ancient. What makes war is still the same.

21

SCIENCE TO THE RESCUE

SO WE can understand ourselves and this age when people say that it is materialistic. The taunt about "a quart of milk a day for Hottentots" is a canard thrown in Vice-President Wallace's face by isolationists: but basically it is true of all modern thinking. I am for Wallace and for world co-operation, but not for "a quart of milk. . . ." For there could be no better vision of world peace for this Age than a quart of milk a day for everybody, particularly pasteurized milk. Raising the standard of living is the utmost we can conceive of. It almost seems to say, "Give a fellow a quart of milk a day, and he will be a good man, a just man, and a free and contented man. Give the world a quart of milk a day, and it will be a good world, a just world, and a free and contented world. If there are only enough cows and timothy grass, the problems of world peace are solved."

So now the money-changers have converted God's temple into a Stock Exchange, and the smell of metallic lucre has blended with the smell of the cedars of Lebanon. That was what so annoyed Jesus and made him take out his whip of cords. I wonder that it does not annoy the followers of Christ. I know that there is a philosophy of living among the people of any land, with or without Christianity; no nation ever existed, or could exist, without its *mores,* or its body of moral tradition. The Chinese believe, "The four moorings of the ship of state are: courtesy, justice, integrity and sense of honor." [36] In Christian lands, this body of moral tradition takes the form of Christianity. But the world is shifting; scientific materialism

---

[36] Saying by Kuantse, seventh century B.C. The book ascribed to him was probably composed or interpolated several centuries later.

has cut Christian faith from under. Christianity has nothing to do with modern politics or business, and it is politics and business that are shaping our lives. The case of the world is a case of belief versus disbelief.

The search for belief is everybody's business, for in a world of international chaos following the disappearance of belief, the scientist is affected as much as the preacher. In a shipwreck the engineer sinks with the stoker. It is as much the scientist's business to inquire about man's faith as it is the preacher's to inquire about science, for both are merely searching for some meaning in life, some sustaining faith. The restitution of the values of human life is the first job of modern man's intelligence.

The rainbow has been dissected, the childhood wonder and fancy have gone, and the world has gone gray with us. Yet has the wonder gone? The public as little understands science as it understands the vitamin pills which it takes every day. In a great scientist, curiosity has never killed wonder. For today it is science itself that has opened up the world of wonder, and curiosity arouses a greater, unquenchable curiosity. Great knowledge always brings humility. Today it is great doctors who confess to you privately that they don't know how diseases are cured, and it is the greatest scientists who tell you they don't know what is matter and why it behaves the way it does. The verification of processes has not helped the inquiry into primary causes or objectives. The study of the color of butterfly wings has only made the problem more complex than before; electron microscopes have shown tiny skyscrapers erected on the wings' surface with floors built so that their height corresponds with the wave length of blue or violet rays. Science never tells you who builds these microscopic skyscrapers, or who tells the butterfly to do so. The arrival of the fittest seems harder than ever to explain, and the Darwinian concept of chance variations must sound unconvincing and fall to the ground. Today it is science that will teach us humility.

On the basis of humility alone will science and religion be reunited.

But more than that, science is destroying matter and therefore destroying materialism itself. Science starts out with mathematics to examine the universe and is now returning the universe to mathematics. The wise scientist has pretty well washed his hands of matter. He has reduced liquids, solids, light, color, smell, sound, and all the physical properties of matter to certain mathematical formulas—*beyond which there exists nothing that he knows, or claims to know.* A solid table has become empty space; an atom is like a half-mile-long jai-alai stadium without walls in which tiny balls swirl about, and a molecule is like a series of open-air jai-alai stadiums, held together without visible or material adjoining walls. A conglomeration of matter is only a "field" of action, and the balls themselves have neither mass nor volume. Matter itself has been spirited away, and the laws of matter no longer operate in the core of things of this universe. The universe is more like a ghost than like a machine. And so the scientists themselves have become less "materialistic" than the great of the Stock Exchange.

But the destruction of the conventional notion of matter at once involves also the destruction of the nineteenth-century mechanistic concept of the universe. It is interesting to note that Sir James Jeans, in his latest book, *Physics and Philosophy,* also strikes upon the problem of determinism versus free will as influenced by the changing concepts of matter itself. While his attitude is strictly "scientific" and he is hesitant in drawing conclusions about the end of "materialism" and "determinism," calling it mainly a question of terminology, he does say,

> At least the new physics has shown that the problems of causality and free-will are in need of a new formulation. . . . The classical physics seemed to bolt and bar the door leading to any sort of freedom of the will; the new

physics hardly does this; it almost seems to suggest that the door may be unlocked—if we could only find the handle. The old physics showed us a universe which looked more like a prison than a dwelling-place. The new physics shows us a universe which looks as though it might conceivably form a suitable dwelling-place for free men, and not a mere shelter for brutes—a home in which it· may at least be possible for us to mould events to our desires and live lives of endeavor and achievement. . . . [Whether we continue to call matter "matter" or not] what remains is in any case very different from the full-blooded matter and the forbidding materialism of the Victorian scientist. His objective and material universe is proved to consist of little more than constructs of our own minds. In this and in other ways, modern physics has moved in the direction of mentalism.[37]

If scientific materialism and Darwinian naturalism of the nineteenth century colored man's mind and produced in the course of time political and economic materialism, so it is inevitable that today science's repudiation of the conventional notion of "matter" must also in the course of time color man's mind, cause a slump in materialistic values, and completely alter the mechanistic qualities of the thinking of this age. Someday we shall speak of "fields" of moral action and attraction and the "time-space-continuum" of historical development, in which not a particle of matter ever operated in history's judgment. In such a world, only "ideas" without mass or weight or volume will be accounted as real. So must man's mind be made in the image of the universe he knows. Science is spiritualizing the whole universe, but it takes years to produce the philosophic effect.

But science has not only destroyed the traditional concept of matter; it has produced a concept of relativity, whose full

---

[37] *Physics and Philosophy* by Sir James Jeans (Macmillan, 1943) pp. 215-216.

philosophic import will not be made plain until decades from now. Relativity is merely the road to mysticism through mathematics. By grappling with the ultimates of time and space and motion, it has struck at their very foundations; by holding or assuming that space is curved and time probably the borrowed embodiment of motion in our minds, both being in fact mathematically interchangeable with motion itself, it has brought us closer to a theory of the rhythm of life.

At last, the pulse beat of the universe is better understood. The straight line, square space, and rectilinear time are the last conventions of thinking to be exploded by science, following the explosion of the myth of the flat earth. If the universe is not infinite, it must be round, and cannot be square. But if the universe itself is round, there can be no absolute straight lines, for every straight line curves invisibly. Briefly, this "roundness" is as incomprehensible to us as the roundness of the earth must be to two ants crawling on two parallel longitudinal lines somewhere in Wisconsin, both making for straight north. With the roundness of the earth, the Far East has actually become the Far West of America, and an Eskimo going steadily north will strike upon Australia or New Zealand. The same thing must be true of the lines and directions of a round universe, of which the earth is considerably less than a suggestion of a microscopic speck.

The universe therefore consists only of circles and their modifications. Any "circulist" picture (my own term) will present a better and truer picture of life and motion and material objects than a cubist picture. Cubism is scientifically incorrect; even light impulses move in waves. In the very pointed lines of cubism, I see only the harshness of the modern spirit.

And so the true historian can draw a picture of human history only in curves also, with constant emerging and submerging and blending of cycles. The Chinese Taoists knew this well; the whole *yin-yang* concept was based upon the wave theory. Emerson in his essay on "Circles" understood this principle of life also. The ultimate mysticism of the universe is the rhythm of life which annihilates all distinctions, or as Chuang-tse put it in his famous essay, "the levelling of all things." As East and West and North and South lose their absolute meaning through perception of the roundness of the earth, so life and death, growth and decay, strength and weakness, big and small, and all hard-and-fast distinctions become relative in an all-comprehensive all-levelling philosophy of relativity.

The winter begins strictly on summer solstice, when the days begin to shorten, and the summer begins strictly on winter solstice, when the days begin to lengthen: this is the philosophy of alternate cycles and the hidden "germ," on which the whole Confucian "Philosophy of Mutations" (*Yiking*) is based. The hidden germ (*chi*) and the manifest (*chu*) merely alternate, and the wise can foretell the future from the present alignment of proceeding and receding, or dominant and recessive, forces. The apple tree begins to die when it reaches its greatest flowering splendor, and the prime of power is the beginning of decay. The generations of men are not joined to each other like a string of sausages, but one begins while the other is in its prime, merging with it like the invisible curves of a woman's body. So also rise and decline in waves the generations of the thoughts of men. All life is like the ocean waves on a seashore to one who observes them closely; they recede while appearing to proceed and the water goes up when the crest begins to fall.

From this arises the contempt for all philosophic absolutes. Such a philosophy destroys all Euclidean mathematics. Relativity is a philosophy of life as well as a mathematical formula for explaining the universe. Only recently has science grown big enough for the theory of Relativity. But thousands of years ago Taoist sages, particularly Laotse and Chuangtse, jumped the mathematics, and by sheer breadth of vision and profundity of insight reached and anticipated its philosophic meaning—the relativity of all standards.

For this may be regarded as a summary of the cold skeleton of Chuangtse's philosophy regarding Relativity. "Dimensions are limitless; time is endless. Conditions are not constant; terms are not final." [38] All standards are relative to the point of view of the onlooker.

> In regard to distinctions, if we say that a thing is great or small by its own standard, then there is nothing in all creation which is not great, nothing which is not small. To know that the universe is but as a tare-seed and the tip of a hair is [as big as] a mountain—this is *the standard of relativity*. In regard to function, if we say that something exists or does not exist by its own standard, then there is nothing which does not exist, nothing which does not perish. If we know that east and west are convertible, and yet necessary, terms in relation to each other, then such [relative] functions may be determined.

The exact words for "relativity of standards" are "levelling of standards or gradations," but the philosophic meaning of the dependence of standards is quite apparent. The distinctions of high and low are likewise annihilated; the nadir is the beginning of the upward curve and therefore philosophically the highest point, the zenith is the beginning of the descending curve and philosophically the lowest. "To Tao, the zenith is not high, nor the nadir low; no point of time is long ago; nor by the lapse of ages has it grown old." The distinction between *this* (subjective) and *that* (objective) is relative, both being dependent on the speaker.

> Hence I say, "this" emanates from "that," and "that" also derives from "this." *This the theory of the interdependence of "this" and "that"* . . . when "this" (subjective)

---

[38] *Wisdom of China and India*, p. 683. For following quotations from Chuangtse, see pp. 685, 636, 637, 631.

and "that" (objective) are both without their correlates, that is the very "Axis of Tao." And when that Axis passes through the center at which all Infinites converge, affirmations and denials alike blend into the infinite One. . . . [Therefore] only the truly intelligent understand *this principle of levelling of all things* into One. They discard the distinctions and take refuge in the common and ordinary things. The common and ordinary things serve certain functions and retain the wholeness of nature. From this wholeness, one comprehends, and from comprehension, one comes near to the Tao.

Hence there is a Balance of Heaven according to which parallels meet.

A keeper of monkeys said with regard to their ration of nuts that each monkey was to have three in the morning and four at night. At this the monkeys were very angry. Then the keeper said they might have four in the morning and three at night, with which arrangement they were well pleased. The actual number of nuts remained the same, but there was a difference owing to [subjective evaluations of] likes and dislikes. It also derives from this [principle of relativity]. Wherefore the true Sage brings all contraries together and rests in the natural Balance of Heaven. *This is called [the principle of following] two courses [at once]*.

Hence all values are submerged, all distinctions are leveled, all judgments are relative to the onlooker's point of view, and all "material transformations" (*wu-hua,* an important concept in Chuangtse) are part of the cycle of life. The frog in the well is proud of his little puddle, the River Spirit is proud of his little autumn flood, the summer insect who knows not winter discusses ice, the lake sparrow cannot understand why the giant roc has to fly five thousand miles, Peng Tsu is proud of his long life of eight hundred years, the screech owl is proud of the dead rat in its claws, and little men are proud of their power and success! Therefore it is said, "The perfect man ignores self; the divine man ignores achievement; the true Sage ignores reputation." From such an understanding of the relativity of all standards and of the cycle of life, the basis for contention and the belief in force is destroyed. Man finds his final repose in Tao, or knowledge of this cycle. "The Great [universe] gives me this form, this toil in manhood, this repose in old age, this rest in Death. Surely that which is such a kind arbiter of my life is the best arbiter of my death." [39]

Such a spiritual softening of man's thinking and wisdom must come about; the crudities of a mechanistic belief in material, rectilinear absolutes must be worn off and made to disappear; action must be judged in waves and ripples and emerging and submerging cycles, and to do this, a longer range must be taken, so that what appears to be a straight line may be seen to be a curve, and what appears a curved line may turn out to be the shortest route between two points. Nature herself is gentle and travels by waves, in the figure "S," circle interpenetrating continuing circles, and in spite of obstacles goes on. Nature always bends. Believers in power and direct action who think that they are "thinking straight" are poor students of Nature.

Therefore, following nature, according to Laotse:

> To yield is to be preserved whole,
> To be bent is to become straight,
> To be hollow is to be filled,
> To be tattered is to be renewed. [40]

[39] *Ibid.*, p. 659. Emerson's essay on "Circles" is worth very careful study. His deductions about the rhythm of life and his difficulty in facing the practical outcome of "inaction" are very similar to Chuangtse's. He was the first American relativist.

[40] *Ibid.*, p. 594. For following quotations from Laotse, see pp. 587, 586, 623, 608, 609, 599, 600, 615, 623, 618, 601, 624, 623.

Believers in brute force, like Hitler, always take the logical, direct line, and this is why they run counter to nature and when a material obstacle meets their path, they have no escape and are destroyed. Laotse and Chuangtse have the knack of making Hitlers and would-be Hitlers of the world appear unphilosophical and foolish. Every structure of force crumbles, irrespective of who builds it.

> Stretch [a bow] to the very full,
>   And you will wish you had stopped in time.
> Temper [a sword-edge] to its very sharpest,
>   And the edge will not last long.

Thus it is easy to see that from such a relativist and "circulist" philosophy, as against western traditional absolutism, certain remarkable changes will follow in man's outlook upon life. Such a philosophy has already produced changes in Chinese daily behavior to an extent that justifies its being called "ways that are dark" by westerners. It seems strange that whether you are a circulist or a believer in the impossibly naïve rectilinear values of the West should make such a vast difference in your mental outlook, but it does. It affects your view of yourself, your fellow men, the way you meet fortune or disaster, and politics and peace itself.

The first result is that it immediately abolishes the goosestep, and you learn to travel in the figure S, like a skater. You develop a certain deviousness of approach to problems, like a desire to hide in obscurity and avoid the spotlight, but you also gain a certain inner strength in meeting contingencies, on the belief that. "Disaster is the avenue of fortune, and fortune is the concealment for disaster." You learn to be a little less direct and more subtle; you feel even a little happy when you know you are being taken advantage of, because you know that the man who likes to take advantage of others is bound to end up by being friendless. You develop an enormous patience with fools.

The second result of this relativism is that you end up in Laotsean paradoxes. From the Chuangtsean "levelling of all distinctions," you naturally reach the Laotsean inversion of all values. You begin to lose your faith in power and force and insolence and arrive at the Doctrine of Weakness as the strongest thing in the world. And you begin to believe the following Laotsean paradoxes and imbibe a little of the Laotsean humor:

> The best of man is like water;
>   Water benefits all things
>   And does not compete with them.
> It dwells in (the lowly) places that all disdain,—
>   Wherein it comes near to the Tao.

> That weakness overcomes strength
> And gentleness overcomes rigidity,
> No one does not know;
> No one can put into practice.

> The greatest cleverness appears like stupidity;
> The greatest eloquence seems like stuttering.
> Movement overcomes cold,
> (But) keeping still overcomes heat.

> The good ones I declare good;
> The bad ones I also declare good.
>   That is the goodness of Virtue.
> The honest ones I believe;
> The liars I also believe.
>   That is the faith of Virtue.

The third result, which follows from the above, is that you develop a contempt for force and conquest, because the strongest army breaks first, even as Hitler's or Napoleon's did. As an ancient Chinese proverb says, "The violent man shall die a violent death." If Nature is soft and goes in curves, the man who believes in force and direct action does not comprehend even the laws of the universe he is living in. Therefore:

When the world lives in accord with Tao,
Racing horses are turned back to haul refuse-carts.
When the world lives not in accord with Tao,
Cavalry abounds in the countryside.

Therefore a good general effects his purpose and stops.
  He dares not rely upon the strength of arms;
Effects his purpose and does not glory in it;
Effects his purpose and does not boast of it;
Effects his purpose and does not take pride in it;
  Effects his purpose as a regrettable necessity;
  Effects his purpose but does not love violence.
(For) things age after their prime.
That (violence) would be against the Tao.
And he who is against the Tao perishes young.

I have no doubt therefore that Laotse's solutions for the problems of the relationship between big and small powers and for the peace settlement are the only ones that are basically sound and lasting:

A big country (must be like) the delta low-regions,
  Being the concourse of the world,
  (And) the Female of the world.
The Female overcomes the Male by quietude,
And achieves the lowly position by quietude.

Therefore if a big country places itself below a small
  country,
  It absorbs the small country.

(And) if a small country places itself below a big
country,
It absorbs the big country.

Therefore some place themselves low to absorb
(others),
Some are (naturally) low and absorb (others).
What a big country wants is but to shelter others,
And what a small country wants is but to be able
to come and be sheltered.
Thus (considering) that both may have what they
want,
A big country ought to place itself low.

In a truly civilized peace treaty, the "guilt clause" will be
abolished. For according to Laotse:

Patching up a great hatred is sure to leave some
hatred behind.
How can this be regarded as satisfactory?
Therefore the Sage holds the left tally,
And does not put the guilt on the other party.
The virtuous man is for patching up;
The vicious is for fixing guilt.
But "the way of Heaven is impartial,
It sides only with the good man."

Only at a peace conference where both opponents insist on
fixing the guilt on oneself will there be permanent peace.

The fourth and last result is that, knowing the law of the
cycle of life, man would seek to live in harmony with that universal law, thus avoiding ruin for himself and reaching that
truly religious level which comes from comprehension of the
universe itself.

I have Three Treasures;
Guard them and keep them safe:
  The first is Love.
  The second is, Never too much.
  The third is, Never be the first in the world.

Through Love, one has no fear;
Through not doing too much, one has amplitude
    (of reserve power);
Through not presuming to be the first in the world,
  One can develop one's talent and let it mature.

For love is victorious in attack,
  And invulnerable in defense.
Heaven arms with love
  Those it would not see destroyed.

Curiously, through such a world outlook, which is the very antithesis of the doctrine of power, Laotse arrived at an absolutely identical position with Jesus, not only with regard to "not requiting evil with hatred," but also in the following truly religious perceptions:

The Heaven and Earth join,
  And the sweet rain falls,
Beyond the command of men,
  Yet evenly upon all.

He lives for other people,
  And grows richer himself;
He gives to other people,
  And has greater abundance.

Who receives unto himself the calumny of the world
  Is the preserver of the state.
Who bears himself the sins of the world
  Is the King of the World.

Somehow the laws of the moral universe have been discovered independently in Asia Minor and Asia Major and ultimately agree. And both seem to revel in paradoxes a little too subtle for the goose-stepping modern scientific man.

A hurricane cannot last long, says Laotse; modern civilization is a hurricane. Only by some such dulling of the edges and softening of the corners of man's thinking can the present civilization, faced with growing sharp conflicts, be saved. The "dregs and tumors of virtue" have to be cut out. They are disgusting in the sight of Tao.

22

THE SEARCH FOR PRINCIPLES

WE HAVE strayed far into the field of Nature. It is time that we come home and remember that we are men. The only important philosophical question of today is: what are we, and what is man?

When Confucius heard that a stable had burnt down, he asked if any man was hurt, but "did not inquire about the horses." I am such a "humanist" that I do not care if the whole species of horses and dogs and cats and rabbits are wiped out, if man hereafter can live in peace. This may sound a little Oriental and heathenish, but there are, on the other hand, men whose minds are almost as limited in compass as mine, and who, while very much devoted to the very lovable dogs, have not yet any conception of the brotherhood of *all* men. I am sure horses think the same way, too. The white horses are devoted to man, but have nothing but contempt for brown and bay horses, and the brown and bay horses have nothing but contempt for the spotted ones. Horse love, I understand, is only skin deep. The most inconceivable barriers of pigment exist. In the same way, a bulldog will patronize a human being, but must persecute his brother, the Irish terrier, because his own tail is straight and smooth while the other dog has a wiry tail and somewhat too much of a mustache. How the westerners laugh at Chinese high cheekbones and almond eyes and how the Chinese laugh at the westerners' hairy chests and arms!

But this state of things is not funny any more. We are starting out on an era of compulsory world living with all the tribalistic traits of a past epoch and the psychology of the bull-dog-terrier racial prejudices. We talk lightly of world co-operation and world government without realizing the immense complexities of the new problems, not only in respect of their size, but also in respect of their nature.

Perhaps Aristotle's *Politics* is broad enough, or perhaps it isn't, but a modern Aristotle, his analytical mind exercised over the new problems created by a world state, would ponder very deeply and seek for certain cardinal principles. Aristotle would be what we call a "realist," but his realism would be profound, and he would not necessarily potter around with "expediencies" in ignorance of first principles. He would still classify the three possibilities of the government of the world, like those of a state, as being the rule of the one, the rule of the few, and the rule of the many, but taking the nations instead of individuals as the units. He would still postulate the good and bad forms of each: the good being monarchy, aristocracy, and timocracy; the bad being tyranny, oligarchy, and democracy. And he would picture how these different principles would operate, and speculate how each might degenerate and how each might evolve into, or be replaced by, another form. And he would still apply his psychology of motivation, and would maintain:

In considering how dissensions and political revolutions arise, we must first of all ascertain the beginnings and causes of them which affect constitutions generally. . . .

The universal and chief cause of this revolutionary feeling has already been mentioned; viz., *the desire of equality,* when men think that they are equal to others who have more than themselves; or again, *the desire of inequality and superiority,* when conceiving themselves to be superior they think that they have not more but the same or less than their inferiors; pretensions which may or may not be just.[41]

He would find the two desires, for equality and for inequality or superiority, still operating today in respect of a World Federation and as causing all dissensions or revolutions that may consequently come up. And he would not conceive of any one form of World Government as so perfect, so good, so just, that it would not undergo internal transformations from psychological causes, or even evolve from one form to another by a series of world revolutions. He would rather try his best to see that the best and the most just form be adopted to ensure the greatest stability. Being a knower of human nature and its corruptibility, he would be realistic and would probably despair of a utopian settlement. But his would be a less mechanistic mind than ours, and he would certainly not agree with Ely Culbertson's international contract bridge, or trust a mechanical elaboration of a World Police Force and say to himself, "There is the basis of an enduring peace." On the other hand, having read Locke now, he would at once plunge into a discussion of the principles of coercion and consent, and their manifold reactions. In addition to the forms like world tyranny (rule of one nation), world oligarchy (rule a few rich nations), and world democracy (rule of the many nations), he would also postulate the collapse of all and a reversion to national autarchy, which in view of the present state of nationalistic psychology, might most likely result.

Aristotle would, I am sure, agree with the general principle

---

[41] Aristotle *Politics,* tr. by Jowett (Oxford), p. 148.

that world peace must be enforced by a world police. But he would analyze the problem further in respect of three points: what to police, who are to police, and who are to be policed, and why. Such a dispassionate examination would reveal that certain things can be policed and certain things not. For instance, he would believe that only such laws and traditions as command the general public approval can be enforced by the police, that police power derives from public approval and sense of justice and not from tear-gas bombs or tommy guns, and that policing an unjust order would be the maintaining by force of a state of things due for a change. So he would be careful to point out that before we decide to police and maintain by force something, we have to make clear what that thing is. Whether, for instance, it will be constrained to defend the *status quo* against "acts of rebellion against the World Government." Secondly, he would closely examine the area and the neighborhood to be policed. He would not try to police too much a peaceful neighborhood, but would concentrate on certain gangster sections that in the past have repeatedly upset public order, where the most "muggings" have been going on. Only the principle of historic experience would seem to serve as safe guidance in regard to those to be policed and those selected to do the policing. And in equity, he would be forced to the conclusion that those nations which have in the past most disturbed others, have been most aggressive, most imperialistic, ought to be the policed nations, and those that have observed the principles of good neighbors ought to be the policing nations. Thus he would probably arrive at the astounding conclusion that Eskimos, Javanese, Samoans, Chinese, and Americans, Danes, Swiss, etc. ought to police the Japanese, the Germans, the English, the French, and the Italians. The Spaniards and Portuguese, though having been once in their time bloodthirsty pirates, ought to be given liberal consideration on parole and good behavior.

In view, however, of the "desire of inequality" of the "Big

Powers," such a scheme is obviously unacceptable. There would probably be a sort of compromise, excluding none and based on complete equality for all nations, or it would lose its police character and have the characteristics of an agglomeration of powers. Following such a principle of common consent and common equality, the best solution would be for the World Police to "belong" to no particular nation, as no community police belongs to any socially prominent members of the community. Such a community police may now and then distribute small, private favors to the socially prominent members, such as better lighting on certain streets or shifting "no parking" signs in their favor, since they pay more taxes, but this must be underhanded and the state of things must not become unbearable to the other poorer members of the community or enrage the public sense of justice.

And over all these questions must stand the philosophic question whether the World Government is to be preponderantly *laissez-faire*, according to Rousseau, or preponderantly regimentalized, according to Hobbes; whether it is to be a government by *Polizei*, according to Prussian Nazism, or government by self-government according to Jeffersonian democracy and the old-roguish Chinese. There is so much trouble that could be avoided if we did not poke our nose into it. The point immediately suggests itself, that the greater the area of government, and the more scattered the populations, the less can force be relied upon in government.

The Chinese, having governed their country for four thousand years without lawyers or police, and having had some experience in the matter of governing large areas, would instinctively incline toward Jeffersonian democracy. After all, a nation that believes in government by worship and song, by rituals and music, must be a little stunned by the idea of government by *Polizei*. The Chinese would probably lead the revolt against the *Polizei*, and they have certain ways of dealing with the police. They believe it is their duty to corrupt them by sending the police sergeant a present when his wife gives birth to a baby because he is so obliging as to stand and guard our doors. They have no idea that he is there to guard public order, since public order is already guarded by scrolls of proverbs and public laughter at transgressors—the thief has a bad mother—but they understand he is there to open limousine doors for rich men arriving at sumptuous hotels. They are not rich themselves, but they can also buy the policeman's small favors by pulling him into their house on a hot day and giving him a cup of tea. Just by sheer human experience, they have found that no policeman in the world can resist such corruption. And the Burmese, the Javanese, the Eskimos, the Samoans, the Caucasian villagers, and the Brazilians and the Chileans would join with the Chinese and shout to the French, the English, the Germans, and the Americans: "What the hell! Why do *we* require your police? We ain't got Krupp guns or parachutists here. Why don't you police yourselves? Why don't you try to police Moscow?"

One may make here also a parenthetical remark about America. America has a fair record, not a blameless, but a fair record, in respect of imperialism. The American is too good a democrat to be a successful imperialist. He pats the foreigners on the back and American doughboys pull rickshaws for Hindus out of sheer fun. That is the last thing an imperialist should do. You haven't got the imperialist instinct. You can't fraternize with "natives" and be their masters. The fellows whose backs you pat today will think tomorrow that they are as good as you are, and good-by to your empire! It's rather odd, isn't it, the way humans think? But America has developed enough power, and power is a dangerous thing, and I am winking and blinking to see what she is going to do with that power. America, having come of age, is like a research doctor who suddenly finds himself married to a socialite. "It's the war," the doctor says, trying to explain his marriage. To go on with the research or move in with his socialite wife to cure corns and misshapen

nails for the rich is now this doctor's central spiritual problem
—and this is the only important problem that faces America
today. For America today stands at the crossroads. Be a research doctor, I say.

23

THE COMMON STANDARD FOR MEN

WE HAVE not yet decided what is the nature of man. We
cannot set up a World Federation of man without knowing
what are the constituent units. So far we know only that they
belong to five categories: White, Black, Red, Yellow, and
Brown. What about the White, Black, Red, Yellow, and Brown?
We know next to nothing. Then without a common denom-
inator, how do we expect to put them together and expect such
a conglomeration to work?

The question of racial and nationalistic antagonisms in the
world state must be solved. Apart from its size, World Government faces a problem that no national government faces to the
same degree. Apart from racial and religious differences that
do often exist inside a nation, there is a disrupting force of
well-entrenched and growing modern nationalism, which
would be comparable only to active racial antagonisms in
groups inside a state. But the principles that hold with respect
to racial and religious antagonisms inside a peaceful state cannot be different from the principles for a World Government
torn by competitive nationalisms. The Swiss Republic has been
able to exist with all its internal racial and linguistic groups on
the principles of equity, justice, and freedom for all. Evidently,
common beliefs make a common nation, and only common
beliefs make a common world. Religious beliefs may differ in

a nation, but at least the Jews and Catholics and Protestants in America have certain fundamental beliefs in democratic values and the values of living as a whole, and, furthermore, they are willing all to believe that no one is better than anybody else. *If the world is to function as a unit, the faith must ultimately develop equally that no nation is better than any other nation.*

But what do we mean by "better"? Where is the common standard for all men? Such a faith must first establish that races are equal as human beings, and secondly indicate wherein humanity as such can be distinguished from the beasts. As with individuals, so with nations, equality cannot be proved by standards of intelligence or creative ability or moral integrity. It will have to be a mystic standard, a bland assertion that we are all equal just because we are all men.

In other words, we revert to the somewhat unprovable assumption of "human dignity" if we want to be spiritual, or, if we want to be "realistic," say that we are equal because we happen to be all tail-less bipeds. Whether you believe in the version of "human dignity" or in the version of "tail-less bipeds" depends upon your approach, since one is scientifically verifiable and the other not. For one, the voice of the heart is proof itself of "human dignity"; for the other, it is sheer sentimentality—which explains why the believer in the biped version is always so cynical in other problems of national and world politics. So even the basis of agreement that we are all "born equal" has a practical bearing on other problems. It would make no sense for the biped to be particularly noble to his neighbors. The believer in the innate dignity of all men would scorn the biped's naturalism, while the biped believer would call the other's theory moronic sentimental rubbish. What is to be our standard, and which is right?

It happens there is a tremendous amount of "moronic sentimental rubbish" in the Chinese philosopher, Mencius, who not only believed in the innate goodness of man, but believed also in man's essential spirituality and that on this basis of spirituality alone, all men are equal. Mencius was therefore able to evolve a theory of the common dignity and humanity of man, which the Chinese nation as a whole has accepted, for he ranks next only to Confucius. Mencius clearly and adequately established the common standard for all men. The "equality" of man was not mystical, or based on a theological structure. It had even nothing to do with over- or under-pigmentation.

Mencius wanted to establish the common standard of all men and distinguish man from the beasts, a difference which, he pointed out again and again, consisted of an extremely small margin. Since the margin is admittedly so perilously small, even in modern days, we have reason to listen carefully. I am in fact a little desperate and am willing to listen to any theory of any other philosopher who can tell us in clear, unmystical and nontheological terms why he thinks man is not a beast. All the scientific learning of the past century has tended rather to make us think or strongly suspect that in fact, after all, we are beasts and little else, and we are clinging to the notion of human "dignity" obstinately just by ignoring our professors and refusing to listen to reason. Can anyone give a good, nontheological reason?

Mencius was puzzled by the behavior of a beggar, and by a curious human phenomenon: that all animals love life as the highest value, but men sometimes spurn it. (Mencius, I think, is wrong about the animals.) His inference was that there was a higher value for man than animal survival, and furthermore that *all* men shared this value.

A man's life or death may sometimes depend upon a bamboo basket of rice and a bowl of soup, but if you say to a starving man passing by, "Hey, Mister!" and offer it to him with insults, he will refuse to take them; or if you offer them to a beggar with a kick, the beggar will not receive them.

Therefore, Mencius says,

> I love life, but there is something that I love more than
> life, and therefore I would not have life at any price. I
> also hate death, but there is something that I hate more
> than death, and therefore I would not avoid danger at any
> price. If there is nothing that man loves more than life,
> then would he not permit himself to do anything in order
> to save it? And if there is nothing that man hates more
> than death, then why does he not avoid dangers that could
> be avoided? And so there are times when a man would
> forsake his life, and there are times when a man would
> not avoid danger. *It is not only the good men who have
> this heart (or feeling) that there are times when they
> would forsake life and would not avoid danger. All men
> have this heart, only the good men have been able to pre-
> serve it.*[42]

The Mencian standard of common humanity is, in one word,
that there is a *common heart in man,* or in our phraseology,
all races have essentially the same hopes, aspirations, joys, and
sorrows, and that it is these common feelings that unite us,
and establish our essential equality. Then he goes on to prove
how men as a species are psychologically the same, which
makes a common standard in tastes, sounds, and the sense of
right and wrong possible. Proceeding from the analogy of
wheat, Mencius says,

> Therefore all who belong to the same species are es-
> sentially alike. Why should you doubt that this holds true
> also of human beings? *The Sages belong to the same spe-
> cies as ourselves.* As Lungtse says, "A man who proceeds
> to make a pair of shoes without knowing the foot meas-

---

[42] *Wisdom of Confucius* (Modern Library), p. 285. For following quotations from
Mencius, see *Ibid.,* pp. 281-282, and *Wisdom of China and India,* pp. 724, 762-763.

urements will at least not end up by making a wicker basket." Shoes are alike because the people's feet are alike. There is a common taste for flavor in our mouths. Yiya [a famous cook] is but one who has discovered our common taste for food. If, for instance, one man's taste for flavors should differ from that of another man, as the tastes of dogs and horses who belong to a different species differ from the human taste, then why should the whole world follow the judgment of Yiya in regard to flavor? Since in the matter of food the whole world regards Yiya as the ultimate standard, we must admit that our tastes for flavors are alike. The same thing is true of our ears. The whole world regards Master K'uang [famous musician] as the ultimate standard, and we must admit that our ears are alike. . . . Therefore I say there is a common love for flavors in our mouths, a common sense for sounds in our ears, and a common sense for beauty in our eyes. *Why then do we refuse to admit that there is something common in our hearts? What is that thing that we have in common in our hearts? It is reason and a sense of right. The Sage is one who has first discovered what is common in our hearts.* Therefore, reason and the sense of right please our minds as beef and pork and mutton please our palates.

Mencius then proceeds to point out four things common to the hearts of men, which establish first the equality of all men with the Sages, secondly the essential identity of all humanity, and thirdly disqualify one from being regarded as "a man" as soon as he loses them.

The heart of mercy is in all men; the sense of shame is in all men; the sense of courtesy and respect is in all men; the sense of right and wrong is in all men.

Mencius proves it in the following manner:

> Even now-a-days, when men suddenly see a child about to fall into a well, they will all experience a feeling of alarm and distress. They will feel so, not that they may thereon gain the favor of the child's parents; nor that they may seek the praise of their neighbors and friends; nor from a dislike of the sound [of the falling child]. *Hence it is that he who has not a heart of mercy is not a man; who has not a sense of shame is not a man; who has not a sense of courtesy and consideration for others is not a man; who is without a sense of right and wrong is not a man.*

Mencius conveniently forgot about pigment, although there were enough racial differences in China to justify his referring to some tribes as talking a "bird language." In fact, he pointed out that two of the most illustrious rulers of China, Emperor Shun and King Wen, were one "an Eastern barbarian" and the other "a Western barbarian," but that both rose to universal leadership through a "common standard" (*i-k'uei*) of moral power. Such convenient forgetfulness about pigment seems to make it easy for the nations of the world, whether "United" or not, to develop some fundamental faith in racial equality. He did not even mention the standards of industrial capacity or the modern standards of living. By these standards of pigment, industrial capacity, and standards of living we can never be equal.

For what are the standards of living and are they not changing almost every decade? Did the Barretts of Wimpole Street have enamel bathtubs? Did Dr. Johnson ever use a flush toilet or have any idea of a sanitary latrine? Did Charles Dickens ever hear a radio? Did Goethe ever handle a camera? Did Humboldt ever wash from hot and cold water taps? Did he not wash from an earthen basin and water jug? Was Dryden's

room ever steam-heated or air-cooled or electric-lighted? Did
Charles Lamb ever see Ginger Rogers or use a plastic tooth-
brush? Did Wordsworth ever cross in the Hudson tunnel or
drive on the Merritt Parkway? Did Will Shakespeare ever in
his life read one newspaper, not to speak of going to a movie
once a week or listening to Flagstad? Did he have a copy of
the first English Dictionary, which Dr. Johnson compiled a
hundred and fifty years after him? Did his school bench at
Stratford-on-Avon have a collapsible seat, and was the school-
room well lighted? Did he ever see a dentist on Park Avenue?
And did the "second best bed" he so ungenerously bequeathed
to his wife have Simmons springs? To come down to modern
times, did Thomas Edison ever see Errol Flynn? Did Luther
Burbank ever see Radio City? Did Elinor Wylie see a television
broadcast or Will Rogers see a Flying Fortress? Has Albert
Einstein ever really spoken on a transatlantic wireless telephone? As we laugh at the costumes and manners of the
eighteen-nineties, so posterity will laugh at us only twenty or
thirty years from now. Why must we be the mirror to the
universe? Where are the standards?

The invalid assumptions must fall away, and some common
standard for all humanity must be rediscovered. Mencius
repudiated the biped theory and re-established the common
standard of man by the identity of spiritual values. This stands
as a challenge to this mechanical age.

We have covered some important ground, ignoring the
swine-and-slop economic statistics of a thousand postwar plans,
revealing their utter futility in preventing World War III, and
relating the present world chaos to the disintegration of moral
values and ideas in the modern world. I have tried to show that
this world chaos and inevitable wars and conflicts are related
to our changing ideas of the nature of the universe and the
nature of man. I have tried to show that war is inseparably
related to power politics, power politics to the naturalistic view

of human society, and the naturalistic view of human society to the influence of scientific materialism and determinism upon the human studies and modern thought. The deeper question of war and peace hinges upon what we think of man, whether he is a chemical compound and therefore a slave of mechanical laws of struggle, or whether he has the freedom of the will of which Buddha and all teachers of the past spoke. But the chains of materialism, naturalism, power politics and war are forged so fast that from them the modern man finds no escape. The only knowledge available to us in swine-and-slop economic postwar planning is merely the rearrangement of these chains so that they shall rest a little more easily on the ankles or shoulder blades of the mechanical slave. There is a great deal of scientific specialized knowledge which is very impressive, but the best scientist of peace today is merely an expert in anatomy who in his infinite wisdom tells you where the tactile nerves are the least sensitive and where your hide is the thickest so that when the whip descends, you shall be able to bear it with the least self-pity, and even with some fatalistic cheer under the inevitable mechanical laws of necessity. No scientist pretends to break these chains that are binding the spirit of modern man.

Curiously we have stumbled upon Mencius who, in recovering for us a spiritual concept of man, has provided us with a doctrine of equality of all men, a basis for world co-operation among the races of mankind, and the possibility of freedom. He has given us a more flattering view of man than that of mechanical robots which the thousand scientific idiots of the past century have been trying to tell us that we are. At the cost of repetition, I must say that materialists must continue to fight wars eternally. Materialists cannot end wars or devise a peace. They have not the brains for it. Materialists have not the courage to hope. They are not hoping now.

Funny little man, how he conquers the world and is afraid of a little idea, determinism, as if from it he had no escape! A subtle thought might one day seep into man's mind and lend him an escape. It will be just a little idea, come like a tiny key, which the angels shall send us and which shall gently and easily open the chains of mortal man, and that little key is called Free Will. Then, with that little key, Prometheus shall be unbound.

EPILOGUE

WHAT I have written I have written. In every age, Liberty and Reaction go side by side, and he who would be a soldier of peace had better have discerning eyes. And he who has visions of Peace and sees how she is pushed out of our doors and denied entrance, even though she lingers so close beside our doorsteps, will see her turn her steps, bend her head, and silently walk away. Peace and Power are two jealous women and always refuse to stay in the same house. Our rulers are courting and cavorting with the harlot, and while Peace sees them through the window and hears the mad laughter, the bawdy noisiness, and the clinking of champagne glasses inside, she will turn her steps away and never come. For Peace is a lady, and she comes to our house only when she knows she is loved. But those who are guiding the nations' destinies are hypocrites; they love not her but the wench Power, and she knows it. Therefore her face will be hidden from us until she knows that we love her truly and not the harlot Power.

Therefore I hate the harlot and the men cavorting in her company, because I am thinking of their children. Peace is near, but she will never enter. For a great feast is going on and the champagne flows. My friends are having great dreams, the most fabulous dreams, of their life. Despise not the harlot, either, for she has magic. Men can be drunk with her opulence and her beauty, which set their blood coursing and their nerves

tingling, and then imagine themselves poets or kings while
the intoxication lasts. They are counting the extent of their
empires and the glory of their power. "Why," they say to
themselves, "this time we shall roll up the world and put it
in our pockets." The wine of the harlot Power is intoxicating;
there is a drug in it.

And then the morning will come. The madness of the night
before will have become plain. It was the last night of Nebu-
chadnezzar. The world will collapse around them, bankruptcy
will be declared, and these things they shall see with their own
eyes. An auctioneer will come in to tag numbers on the ancestral portraits; there will be much confusion and noise and a
rough lad will sit and test the bed where the mistress slept the
night before. Then furniture-movers will come in and step
on the carpets with their heavy boots caked with mud; no
heirloom will be spared; the ancestral portraits will be thrown
together higgledy-piggledy with wash pails and mops and sent
to the auction shop. After all is gone and the walls are bare,
their children will walk hand in hand out from the front door,
poor orphans, and leave the door ajar, the disinherited. A new
tenant will move in and start repapering the walls and setting
new chairs by the fireside and say, "A new day begins."

But, Peace, go not away. We have not yet made up our
minds. The men are only beginning to drink the champagne
of Power. Some are slightly tipsy, but others are not. Cry
loudly, soldiers of peace, perhaps she may listen. She may yet
change her mind, if we say to her, "We all want you to stay,
whatever your terms. This is our unconditional surrender. For
we want you to live with our children and bless them with
your gentleness and your plenty."

These are simple words. But, as Emerson says, "The simplest
words—we do not know what they mean except when we love
and aspire." It seems that this cynic generation of power
politicians and intellectual critics, struck by an invisible malady,
has lost the capacity for love and the courage to hope. There-

fore they are impotent and cannot bring us peace. But when the world shall have felt a passion for peace and another generation of men shall have recaptured their courage to love and to aspire, then Peace shall steal unaware into our room, and putting her hands across our eyes from behind, whisper, "Guess who?" And before we know it, when we least expect her, she is there to remain by our fireside and bless us and our children with her presence.